MAHABHARATA

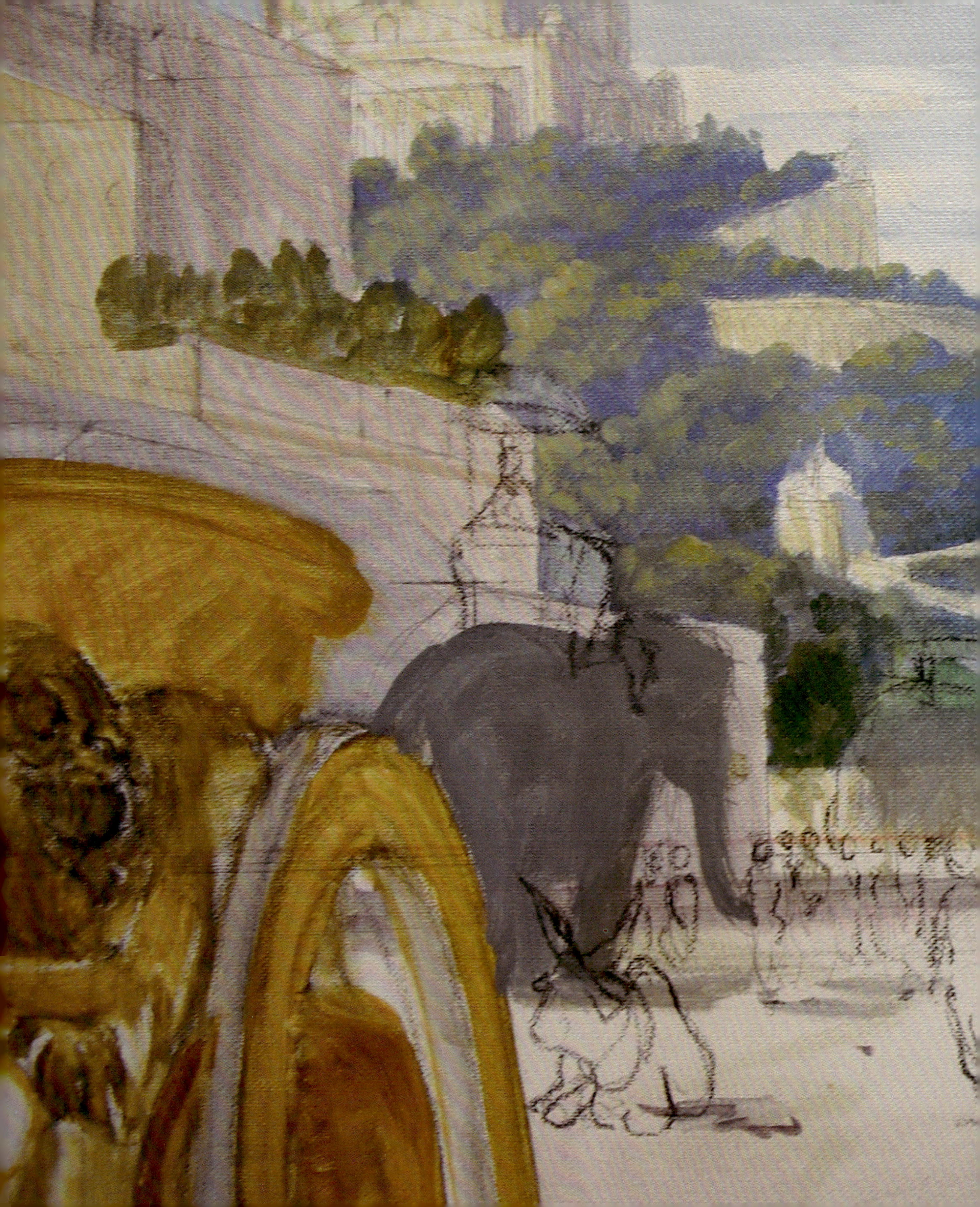

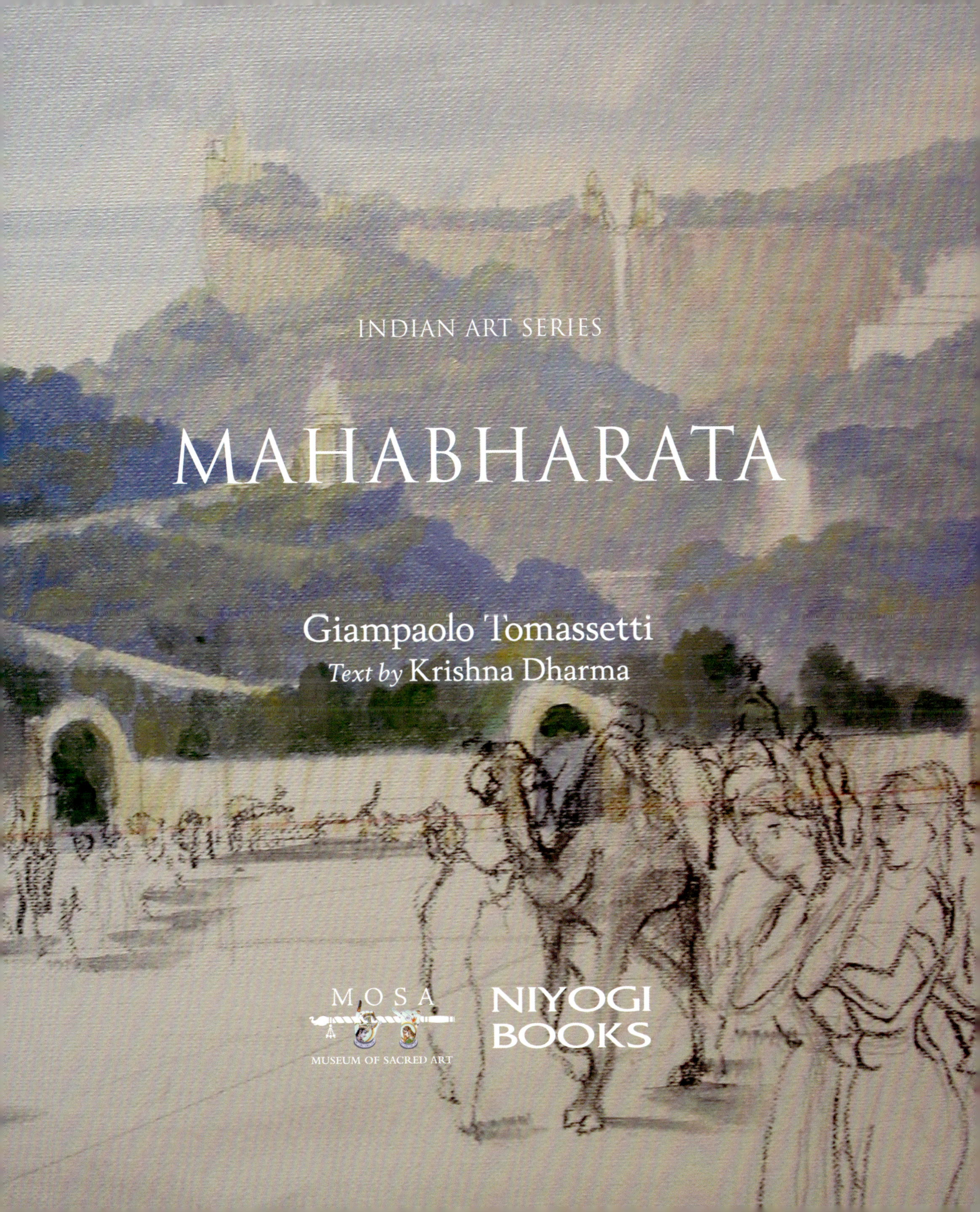

INDIAN ART SERIES

MAHABHARATA

Giampaolo Tomassetti

Text by Krishna Dharma

MOSA
MUSEUM OF SACRED ART

NIYOGI BOOKS

Jointly published by

MOSA
MUSEUM OF SACRED ART

MOSA Belgium
Château de Petite Somme 5,
B-6940, Septon-Durbuy
t: +32 (0)86 43 30 22
e: info@mosabelgium.com
www.mosabelgium.com

MOSA Italy
Via Scopeti 106/108, Florence
San Casciano in Val di Pesa, 50026
t: +39 (055) 82 00 54
e: info@mosaitaly.com
www.mosaitaly.com

NIYOGI BOOKS
Block D, Building No. 77,
Okhla Industrial Area, Phase-I,
New Delhi-110 020, INDIA
Tel: 91-11-26816301, 26818960
Email: niyogibooks@gmail.com
Website: www.niyogibooksindia.com

ISBN: 978-93-85285-14-1
Year of Publication: 2016
First reprint: 2019
Second reprint: 2022
Third reprint: 2026

Printed at: Niyogi Offset Pvt. Ltd., New Delhi, India

CONTENTS

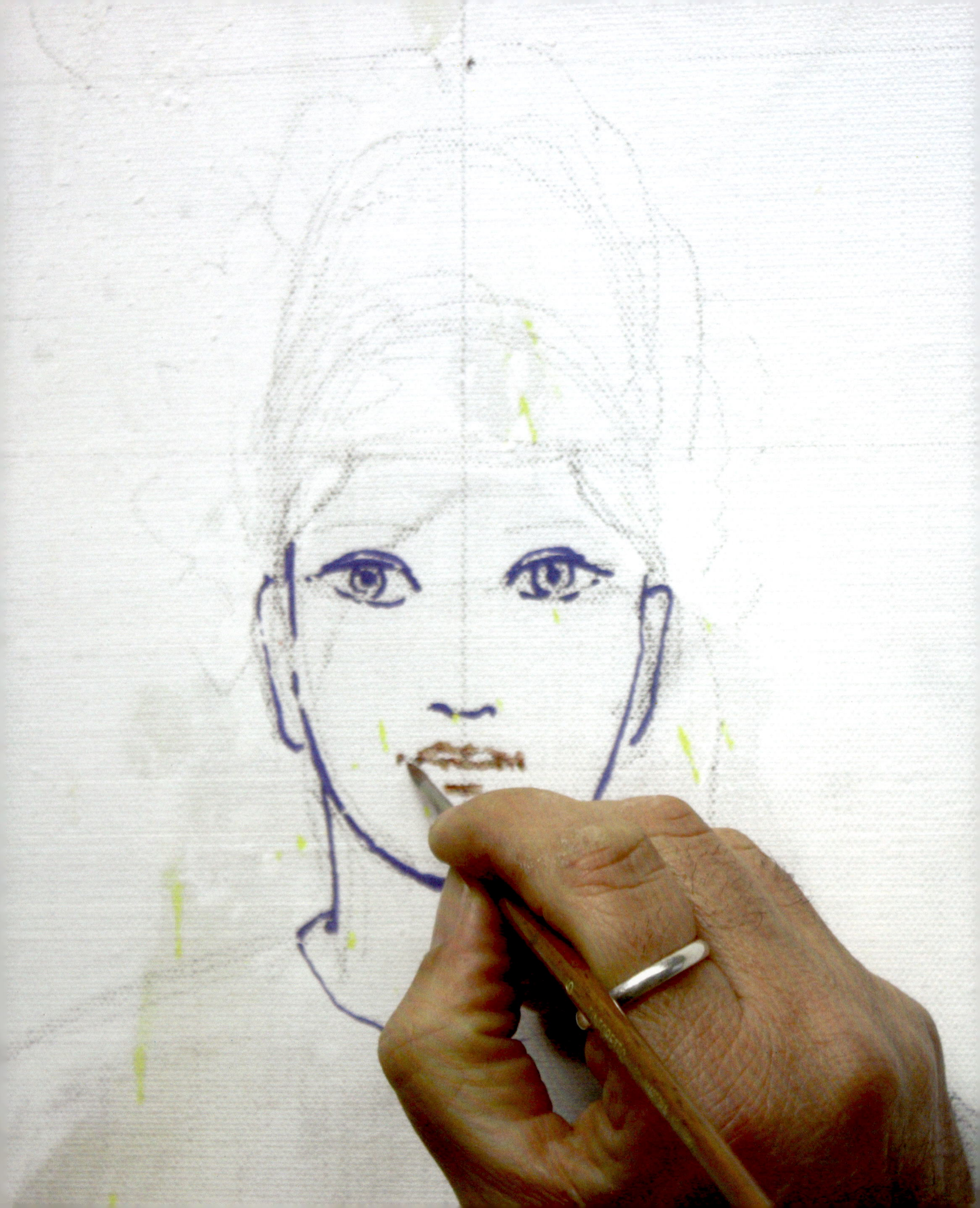

FOREWORD

MOSA purchased the Mahabharata collection by Jananjana Dasa before it miraculously found its way to the ground floor of the main building of Villa Vrindavan, where it is now permanently housed. The works seem to have been made for the walls of the renovated villa, without anyone having been conscious of how this match would take place. Maybe providence played a role. The whole collection perfectly fits in the spacious ground-floor rooms. When I walk through the rooms filled with Mahabharata scenes, I am mesmerized by the size of the paintings and the intensity of the anecdotes and stories they present. They carry us back to a time of great saintly warriors and sages.

This exhibit in Villa Vrindavan, just outside Florence, Italy, marks the opening of MOSA's second branch (its original galleries are in Belgium). MOSA hopes to bring to this beautiful villa in Tuscany a variety of sacred art, including Vaishnava and Hindu art. We are convinced that visitors will cherish their Villa Vrindavan experience: a blend of art, music, dance, spirituality, and amazing vegetarian cuisine.

MOSA renovated Villa Vrindavan's main building to house a permanent collection of ISKCON art based on the great epics Mahabharata and Ramayana and the famous Bhagavat Purana, sacred to all Vaishnavas. Also, MOSA renovated the Villa's old chapel to house temporary exhibits of devotional and sacred art.

I wish to transform Villa Vrindavan into a spiritual experience whose beauty and message touches every visitor. May everyone's heart become purified in this transcendental realm of spiritual devotion.

Some words of gratitude...

To the creator of this amazing collection and his friend who had the vision to carry it forward: Jananjana Dasa and Pandu Putra Dasa – thank you for sharing your passion, talent, vision, patience, tolerance, and joy.

To the leader who is slowly but surely putting Villa Vrindavan on the map of places to visit in Tuscany: Parabhakti Dasa – thank you for your determination and leadership skills.

To the devotees of Villa Vrindavan, who work hard to realize Srila Prabhupada's dream of making ISKCON an exemplary spiritual institution that uplifts humanity – thank you for sacrificing your comfort and security for this higher goal.

Martin Gurvich, Director of MOSA

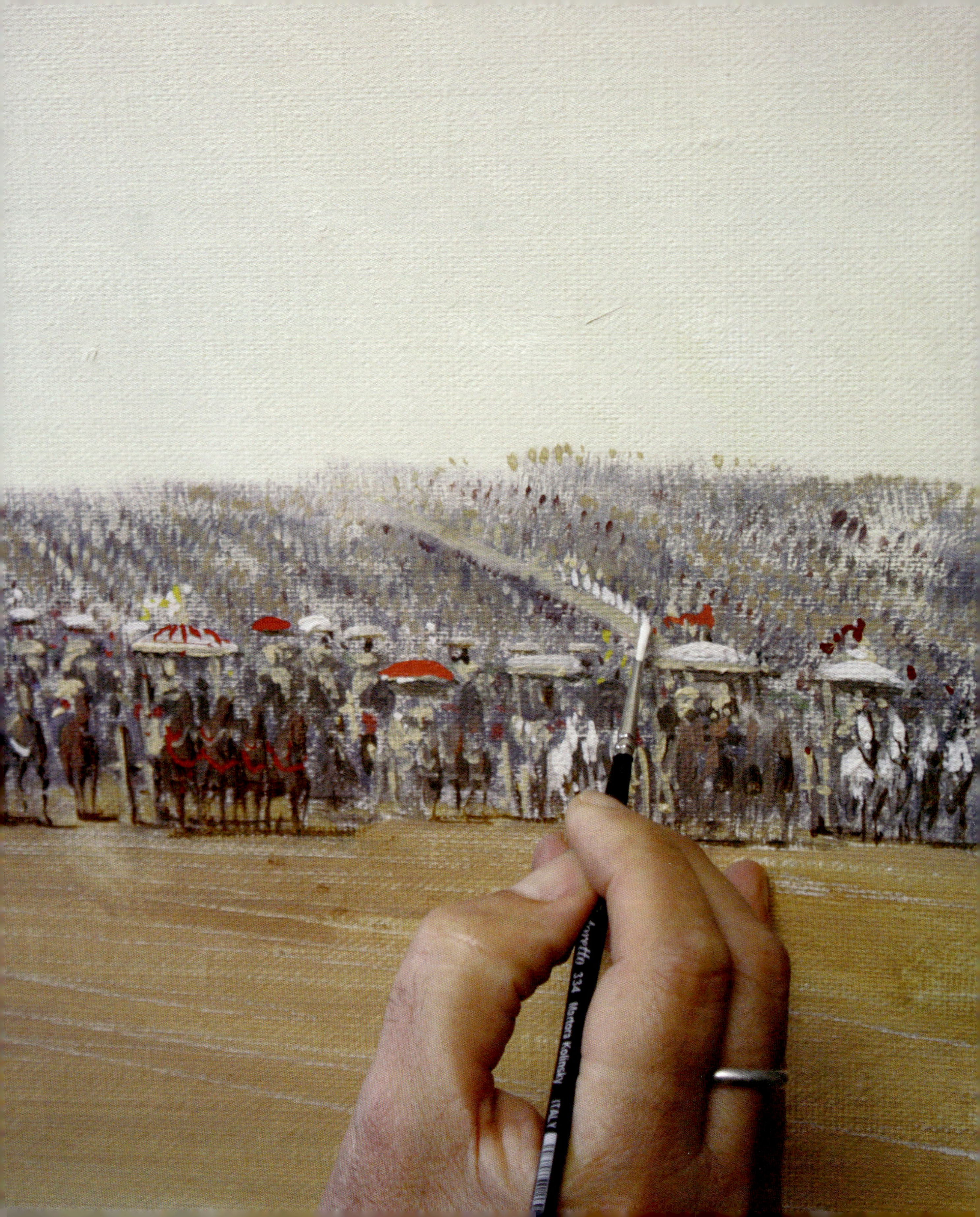

334
ITALY

THE GREAT INDIAN EPIC

Prof. Lokesh Chandra

Mahabharata is a radiant epic that builds on the intensity of the victory of truth over the force of malevolent power. It is the ensoulment of wisdom. An ancient Sanskrit dictum advises that we seek the plentitude of the eternal truths of the Vedas (sruti) in the values of the epics and Puranas (itihasa-puranabhyam srutim upabrinhayet). The epics Ramayana and Mahabharata have both been ways of values, from royal courts to the humblest folk, in the charisma of their narrations and performances, in their depictions as murals and sculptures. This catalogue captures the horizons of sanctity in the charm of paintings.

The sound (sabda) of the epic becomes the form (rupa) depicted by brush. Vyasa's words of imperative evoke the subtlety and richness of our souls. The Mahabharata has been rewritten in literary forms, e.g., in dialogue for performances. It has been painted and sculpted all over Asia, symbolic of the ethos and dynamism of a profound life. This catalogue depicts a modern rendering of its charm and grace, of the nature and nurture of the epic, such that the fratricidal conflict of the Pandavas and Kauravas leads us from the evils of greed to the great hidden values in our hearts.

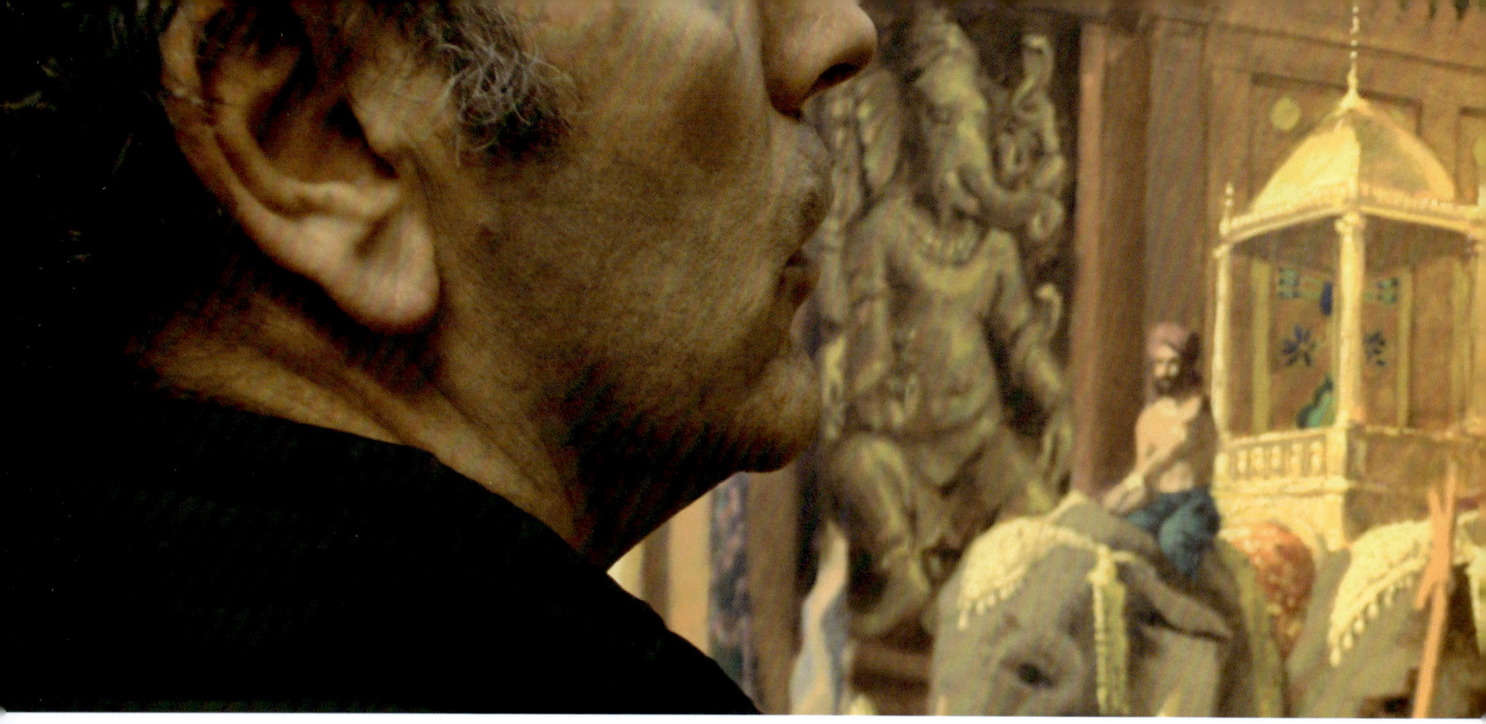

The artist has made an endeavour to reconstitute us into devotion. These paintings are silent poetry, wherein the overflow of splendour awakens the inner being of humans. Their visual form is the unity of a vision (darsana) and experience (sadhana) that becomes a hymn of transcendence. Here any abstract beyond form, or amurata, becomes an icon, or murti. The paintings of the ageless epic become the purity of moonlight, shedding lustre everywhere. These paintings have to be seen as visualisations of perennial social and spiritual values that seek investiture in the subtle and tender summons of life and the yonder universe. The form, or murta, draws humans to their depths, as it stirs the spirit as well as the eye.

The image of the feminine in the Mahabharata reaches the perfection of wisdom and the victory of truth in the person of Draupadi. She is unfettered, outspoken, and independent in the deconstruction of the social conditioning. She incarnates life, to quench the embers of the elders at the royal court of Duryodhana. She is beyond Yudhisthira, a creature of conventions. Yudhisthira stands for law and Draupadi for justice. The Mahabharata frees the victims of psychophysical complexes and leads them to their own transcendence. Draupadi is the serenity of the mind beyond the turbulence of life.

Yudisthira describes her oneiric, dreamlike beauty and yet pawns her, a victim of slumbering forces. As Karna informs her that Yudisthira has lost her

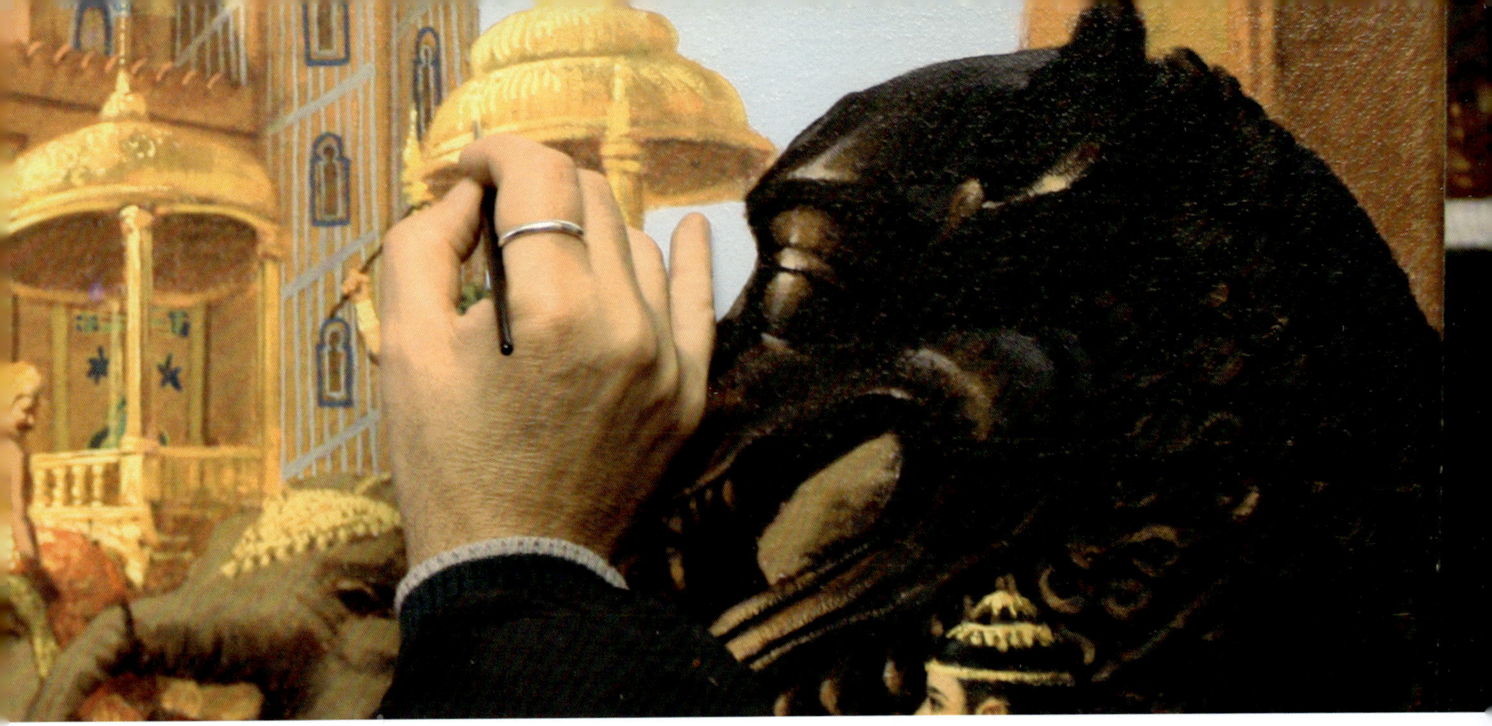

to Duryodhana and that he will now take her to the court, she asks, "Can one who has lost himself pawn me? Can the dharma of social conventions be the dharma of supreme spontaneity?" Karna returns alone, and the royal elders fall silent. Duryodhana orders Duhshasana to bring her to the court. Draupadi wails as they attempt to forcibly disrobe her.

She invokes Lord Krishna, who provides her unending robes. The terror of social logic is replaced by germinative spiritual space. The Kurus are shipwrecked in the stormy sea of the gross world. She sidelines dharmaraja Yudhisthira for dharma Krishna, who steps in to eliminate the disintegrating forces.

This exhibition of paintings is the watershed of the here and now, in which the final word is that dharma emancipates our lives from being lacerated by the reign of hyper-materiality. Here is the moment to create the pure, spiritual dynamism of life. Nothing remains neutral once it is allowed its depths. Sushma K. Bahl and Martin Gurvich lift the veil of fleeting transience and open the lotus of the mind. Our minds soak in our inner fields of dharma and ripen the fruits of enlightenment. This unique exhibition of the great epic represents victory over the insubstantialities of samsara, or repeated birth and death. My admiration goes to this life-giving vision, which flows our way from sublime centuries past.

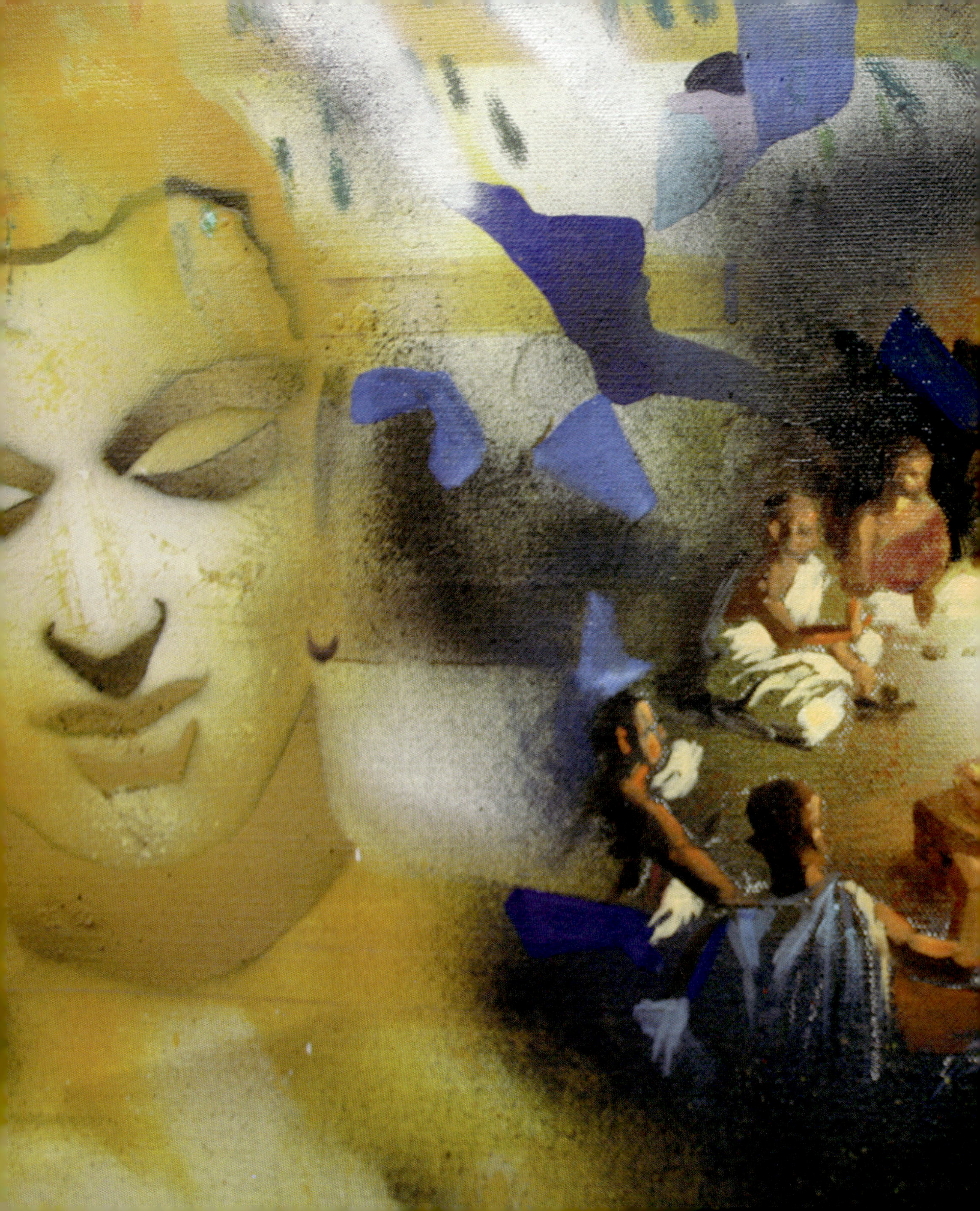

CREATIVE EXPRESSION: MAHABHARATA

Sushma K. Bahl

A series of colourful, creative compositions, inspired by India's Vedic culture, adorning the galleries at Villa Vrindavan, a sixteenth-century mansion in Italy, offers visitors a sublime experience. The painted expressions on display entail stories, symbols, and semblances derived from the ancient Sanskrit epic Mahabharata. Lined with European and Italian Renaissance influences, together with Indian decorative elements and a spiritual ethos, the elaborately drawn and brightly coloured suite articulates the great heroic epic, which is essentially about dharma (moral law). It traverses the struggle for sovereignty between two groups of cousins: the Kauravas (the sons of Dhritarashtra, a descendant of Kuru) and the Pandavas (the sons of Pandu, also Kuru's descendant). The intrigues, struggles, and morals underlined in the spiritual narrative are replayed in amazing dramatic imagery.

Kalakaar (The Artist)

The artist who created the detailed visual re-enactment of the intricate epic narrative is Giampaolo Tomassetti, or Jnananjana Dasa, born and brought up in Italy in a burgeoning middle-class household. His father was an authoritative figure, who worked as a policeman, and his soft-hearted mother was a talented seamstress with a taste for design. Young Tomassetti left home to live on his own while still in his teens, after his handicapped brother and then his mother died in quick succession.

A couple of years of studying philosophy at a university left him looking within. He felt something was missing and wondered who he was. This inner quest, followed by an encounter with members of the Rolling Stones after their concert in Germany, led him onto an artistic psychedelic path. He turned to Oriental philosophy and Indian spirituality and joined The International Society for Krishna Consciousness (ISKCON) in the nineteen seventies. Marriage to another devotee when just twenty required him to earn a living by working as an administrator in a school for a couple of years. But he was more interested in art, and he drew and painted pictures whenever he had some time. It was with encouragement from some American artists who were Krishna devotees that he took to art full-time, as a passion and a profession.

He took art classes and learned to draw, made paintings and murals, produced crafts in clay and wood, worked on frescos, did design graphics, and restored old buildings, learning on the job. "It was all very idealistic and spiritual," recalls the artist. By this time he was known by his spiritual name, Jnananjana Dasa. He worked relentlessly with other devotees to raise one and a half million euros to buy a heritage building that they later named Villa Vrindavan. (It houses the art gallery for this show.) There the artists founded the International Vedic Art Academy. An American couple, Ram Dasa (Kevin Yee) and Dhriti Dasi (Miriam Briks), helped him refine his form. Formal training at an art academy in Florence, which followed, empowered him with theoretical knowledge and the skills to draw anatomy.

The artist took a trip to India in 1981. Traveling for three months there "was an enriching experience, which offered me an opportunity to see and take part in India's spiritual traditions and art practices," says the artist. The Western training had given Jnananjana a sound grounding in realism. It taught him how to use transparent and opaque colours and how to draw landscapes

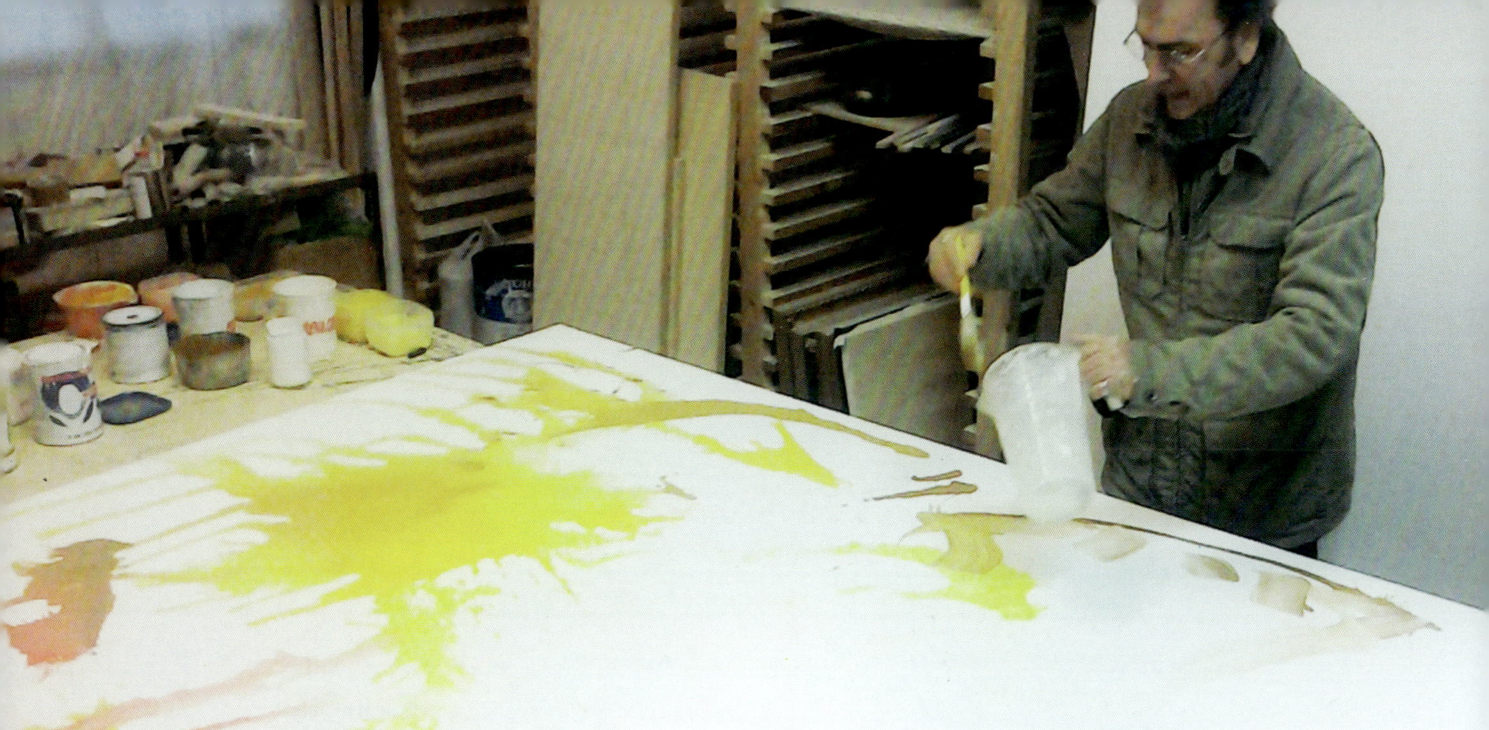

and portraits. The Indian experience enabled him to add decorative elements to his compositions and opened up new possibilities.

A multi-talented artist, Jnananjana is a painter, portraitist, illustrator, muralist, restorer, and fresco artist. He has been engaged in conservation of classical paintings and masters' work. Several of his paintings have been used to illustrate the Bhaktivedanta Book Trust publications. The artist has a rich and impressive repertoire of spiritual art to his credit, including a series of illustrations of Bhagavad-gita in black and white. He has also created paintings based on contemporary themes. Social issues triggered by newspaper reports appear in his collaged work, some of which includes use of organic material like beans and seeds. And he did a sizable series of paintings of horses. His mixed-media art has been exhibited in over thirty solo and group shows all around Italy.

Equipped with the knowledge, confidence and wherewithal to take on an ambitious project, in 2003 he started working on the Mahabharata series. For the last decade his main focus has been the great epic. He has been studying, researching, and meditating on the ambitious project with support from his artist friend, Pandu Dasa, another Italian Krishna devotee, and Martin Gurvich, director of the Museum of Sacred Art (MOSA). His studio at Città di Castello (Perugia) was acquired by Pandu to enable Jnananjana to work on a large scale.

The outcome is reflected in the magnificent series that features episodes of the Mahabharata on an expansive scale. There are twenty-three large paintings in the collection, which visualise scenes of the Mahabharata.

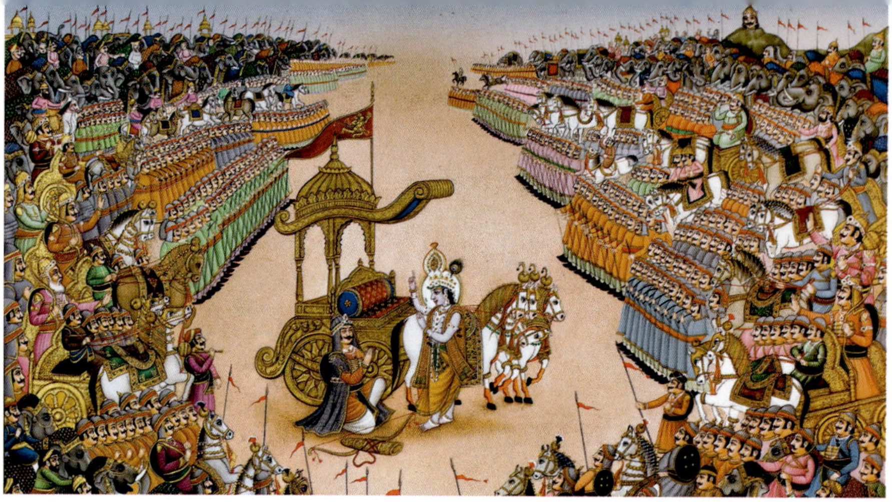

Katha (The Legend)

The epic Mahabharata, eulogised and worshiped by devotees worldwide, takes centre stage in the artist's current creative repertoire. His paintings, mostly in large size and bold colours, engage with the phenomenal Sanskrit epic of ancient India. As the title suggests it is a *mahan* (great) narration about *bharat/baraga* (descendents of Bharat/India), inscribed millenia ago, around 400 BCE by scholarly estimates. Revered as a significant civilizational marker, the Mahabharata is the longest epic poem ever written. In its original, full form, it contains about 1.8 million words in over 100,000 *shlokas* (couplets) or 200,000 plus individual verse lines and long prose passages. The authorship of its primal version is attributed to the sage Vyasadeva. Over the centuries, it has been revised and interpolated in attempts to unravel its historical or compositional layers. It continues to be engagingly mysterious as "re-presented" in the series painted by Jnananjana.

The central plot takes us through the great tale of the Kuru dynasty, the Battle of Kurukshetra, and the fate of the Kurus and the Pandavas. Interlinked is the scripture of Bhagavad Gita, spoken by Krishna, analysed by Indologists in terms of its morals about life, philosophy, goals, and spirituality. The artist elaborates upon all this in evocative compositions. Numerous twists and turns, entailing sequential stories interwoven with free-flowing episodes, are featured in the collection, especially the main characters and issues surrounding the notion of *purushartha* (human duties).

The narrative has been told and retold, chanted and recited, sung and set to music, staged and filmed, made into TV serials and videos, and translated into Hindi, English, French, other languages, and the vernacular languages across India and throughout Southeast Asia and beyond. It continues to be portrayed in numerous miniature paintings and in sculptures in wood, metal, and stone. Mahabharata reliefs adorn various Indian historic and religious sites and Angkor Wat in Cambodia. According to Indologist Wendy Doniger, the epic marks a transitional period, a shift from Vedic sacrifice to sectarian Hinduism and then its interaction with other emerging religions of the time. The Bhagavad Gita and Vaishnava theology, with faith in Vishnu and Krishna, are ingrained in the narrative. Given its relevance across time and space, it is also a source of inspiration in the modern world. The scripture has guided several Indian leaders.

A central theme of Mahabharata is discord in the family. The prime cause was the claim to the throne of Dhritarashtra, the elder of two princes. Owing to his blindness, a ruling was made in favour of his younger brother, Pandu, to become the next king, when their father died. However, Pandu, the heir, was cursed never to father children yet he manages to become the father of five sons – Yudhishtira, Bhima, Arjuna, and the twins Nakula and Sahadeva – whom his wives, Kunti and Madri, beget with the help of demigods. This rules out the possibility of Dhritarashtra's sons inheriting the throne.

After the death of Pandu, the Pandava brothers are forced into exile, along with their wife, Draupadi (made their co-wife to honour their mother's inadvertent comment about her), and then again when Yudhishthira loses everything in a game of dice. On their return home, their envious cousins deny their claim to the throne. So the feud culminates in the famous Battle of Kurukshetra, which took its toll by completely annihilating the Kaurava clan. On the victorious side, the only survivors were the five Pandava brothers and Lord Krishna, who played the role of Arjuna's charioteer and counsel during the battle.

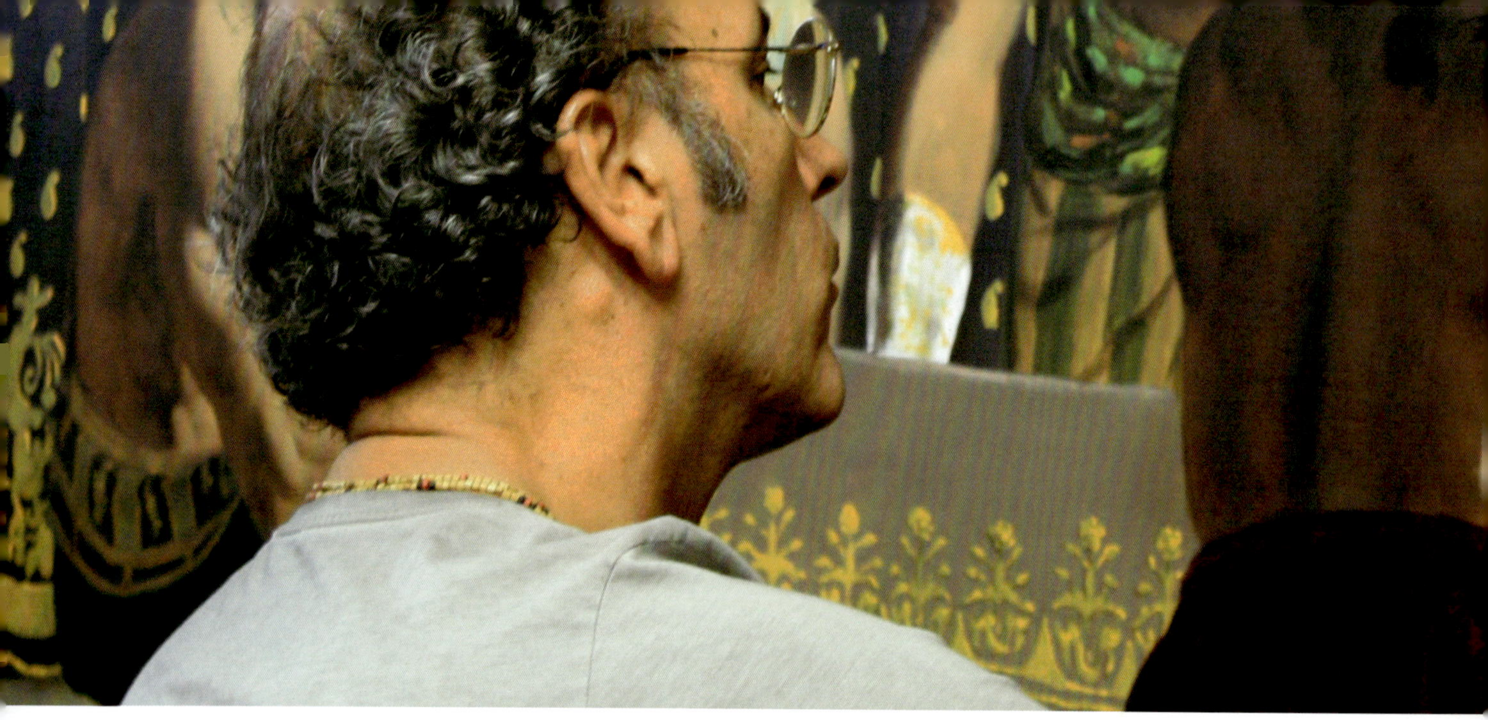

Kalakriti (The Artscape)

Featuring some spectacular composition, the prodigious imagery is painted as if handcrafted, in a mix of techniques, with oil on canvas. The multi-layered work zooms in and out of the fable. It focuses on specific episodes or incidents. The symbols attributed to each iconic form are drawn with a focus on muscles and bones, as prescribed in the artisan's manual known as *shilpashastra*. The display within Villa Vrindavan's galleries, located amidst a Hare Krishna congregation, with its dramatic spiritual and cultural mix, adds to the ambience and appreciation of the artscape.

The collection, centred on the epic Mahabharata, features a wide range of narrations, legends, and divine sites. There are compositions entailing the amazing architectural and scenic grandeur of the holy cities of Dwarka, Indraprastha, and Hastinapur, inhabited by the great civilization. The heavenly beauty of these cities is featured sometimes in aerial views and at other times in an upfront manner and clear perspective. Important occasions and celebrations are drawn in detail and marked in bold colours. The scene in the tent features the Pandava brothers, along with young Abhimanyu, planning their next move at night after a day's fight. The exquisite composition is suggestive of Italian Renaissance work by Caravaggio, and illustrates the artist's ability to play with light and shade. The dramatic chiaroscuro portrayal of the characters in thinking-planning mode and the arrangement around the table highlight the tensions of the moment.

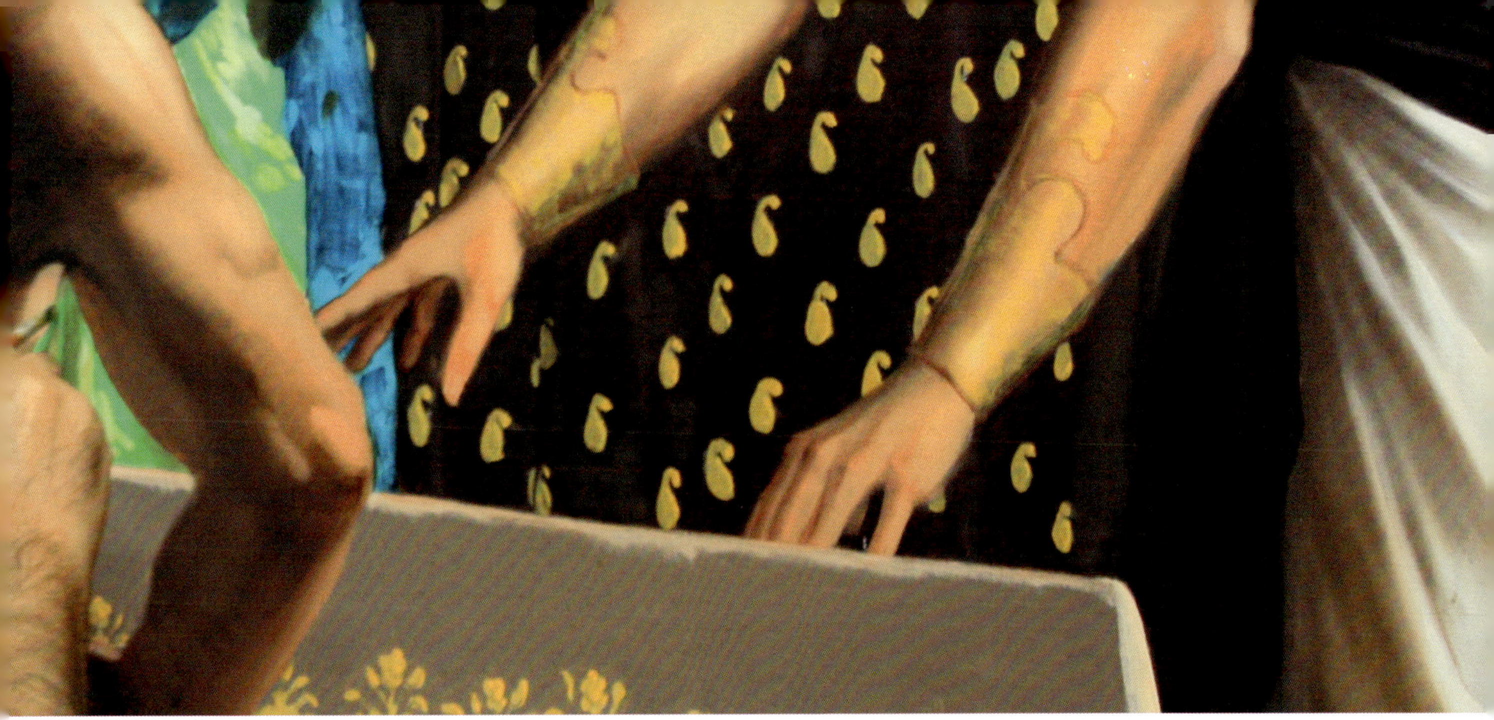

The story of warrior Arjuna's attraction to Subhadra and his taking her away in a chariot provided by Krishna is drawn and painted in immaculate detail. The Vishvarupa avatar of Krishna features mace, disc, club, and blazing brilliance emanating from the divine body, frightening to the sinful and mystical to his devotees. The creative artscape brings alive the arduous trek to Gandhamadana mountain, with its natural beauty, and the deceitful game of dice played by Shakuni, which saw Yudhisthira stake and lose his wealth, kingdom, brothers, and pious wife to the cheats.

The brave warriors, their effulgent costumes, the golden ornaments that adorn the characters, and their chariots or mounts are all meticulously drawn, to signify their persona and status. The amazing depiction of Krishna's pastimes brings a joyful ethos to an otherwise charged atmosphere in some of the paintings. The ferocious battle scene of Kurukshetra, with limbs falling and arrows flying in all directions, is created so realistically that one can almost hear the cries of falling men and dying animals.

Bhima is featured as a great warrior hero, fearlessly fighting a hoard of the enemy army, when his chariot and horses get crushed in the battlefield. Bhima's appearance in another composition presents him in a friendly encounter with Hanuman on his way to a lotus lake in the high mountains. The artist also paints a touching scene between Kunti and Draupadi, who play significant roles in the epic, as they meet for the first time. Equally emotive is the scene where Krishna is featured reassuring Draupadi while she describes her grief over the Kurus' attempt to publically disrobe her.

Numerous plots and themes within the *Mahabharata* are revealed in the artscape. The scripture is a compendium about the code of conduct for kings, warriors, and common people. Such duties are elaborately explained with examples and analogies by Krishna in his dialogue with Arjuna on the battlefield (the Bhagavad-gita). The Mahabharata talks about times of conflict and how individuals should live and face calamity and attain freedom from the repeated cycle of birth and death.

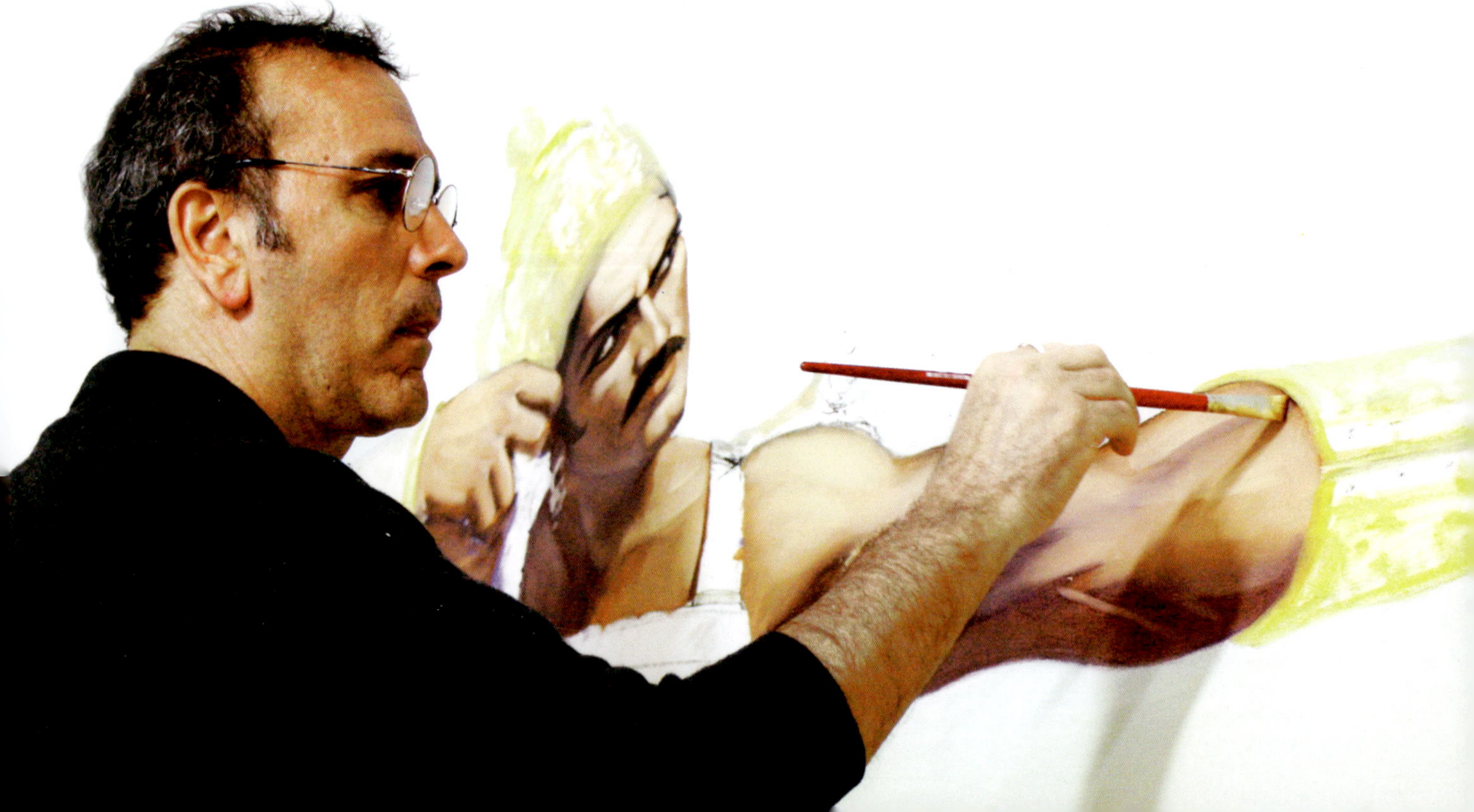

Kalasrishti (The Technique)

Giampaolo Tomassetti/Jnananjana Dasa began his artistic career by making copies and reproductions of old masters' works held in European museums. Photographic reproductions on canvas were touched with oil paint prepared with special glue-gesso, to give the effect of showing cracks, as in old paintings. Gloss was then added to give the works an antique touch. Finally they were encased in wooden frames, with classical floral designs. Making copies of old masters' work was a good learning experience. "This, together with my fresco and restoration work, helped me understand the layers," he says.

The collection is not plain illustration of the narrative. Each painting is focussed on specific elements and the mood of the complex scripture. Familiar subjects and themes are framed and visualised in the artist's personal style, whereby "the mood and psychology of each character," is carefully reflected in the composition.

Jnananjana enjoys the challenge of working on bigger and more complicated paintings. He starts with a prepared canvas or base. It is often a linen cloth with a thin texture. The basic drawing is plotted with charcoal. Then transparent layering of colours is added to give form to the imagery. More layers to add emotions and tones follow. Each work takes between two and five layers, as required. Dark sections are given a transparent colouring treatment, and then opaque colours are added to allow space for light to come through. "Each and every part of the painting is important and nothing is left to chance," explains the artist.

He keeps to the tradition and follows ethnic references in portraiture. Figures are balanced against other forms. Male characters are featured in big-bodied forms, while female characters appear in slender figures. For landscapes and action scenes, Jnananjana takes recourse to spiritual sources and Vedic values. Meticulous attention is paid to the painted surface and imagery, as well as the framing of each work. The framing in earth-coloured wood, with gold leaf and wax coating and drawings on borders, is personalized for each work in classical Western style. It takes the artist months to finish a large painting.

Based on study and research, his work on the epic narrative takes it from legend to reality. Indian decorative traditions are interwoven with Western and Greek artistic elements. They endow the godly figuration, its realistic depiction, with some stylisation. Shadows play a significant role in the compositions. Figures and forms are seen to merge into one another. Sections of the imagery are illuminated with thin lines while the rest is painted in bold colourful strokes.

There is a fine assimilation of East and West in the style, marked for its decorative elements and use of colours. The palette, meticulously chosen and rendered with finesse, adds to his distinct oeuvre. Jnananjana is credited with bringing into the voluminous work a mix of the Vedic transcendental world and a naturalistic, idealistic *brahmananda* spirit. His creative expressions bring alive the classical epic of Mahabharata, a scripture, not a myth but an all-inclusive, felt reality, relevant and pertinent for all times, societies, and spaces as expounded in Mahabharata, Adi Parva 62: ". . . What's here, you can find it elsewhere. But what is not here, there is nowhere."

MAHABHARATA

Kunti and Surya

When Kunti was a young maiden living in her father's palace, the great sage Durvasa once came to visit. Kunti was engaged in his service, and he became pleased with her. So the sage desired to give her a benediction.

By his mystic vision he could see that Kunti would face trying times in her life, and knowing that she would need the gods' assistance, he said, "Dear girl, take from me this mantra by which you can summon any of the gods at your will."

When the sage had departed, Kunti sat upon her bed and began to gaze out of her window. She wondered if the mantra would work. Seeing the sun high in the sky she decided to test it on the sun-god. As she intoned the mantra in accordance with Durvasa's instruction, she suddenly became aware of a dazzling effulgence in the room. She looked up and saw before her the brilliant form of Surya, the sun-god.

He said to her, "Dear Kunti, how may I be of service?"

Kunti gazed in amazement at the god, who had a golden form and was adorned with a sparkling diadem and necklace.

"My lord, I have made a mistake in calling you," she responded. "It was an immature act, and I do not want anything from you. Pray, return to your abode."

Surya replied, "I shall return, but only after fulfilling your desire. I cannot be called in vain."

The splendid looking god said he perceived in her a desire for him: "I shall therefore bestow upon you a powerful child."

Kunti, horrified, cried out, "How can this be? Dear sir, I am but a maiden and cannot give myself to any man before marriage. Please do not sully my virtue."

The god said nothing, and Kunti pleaded with him to forgive her and go. Surya would not relent.

He said, "The other gods will mock me and are already laughing at my plight. Therefore I shall not leave until I have given you a child."

Kunti tried again to change his mind, but he said, "If you do not agree, I shall curse you, your father and the Brahmin who gave you the mantra without considering your immaturity."

Surya said he was already showing her leniency in that instead of punishing her for her foolishness he was offering to give her a son who would be practically his equal.

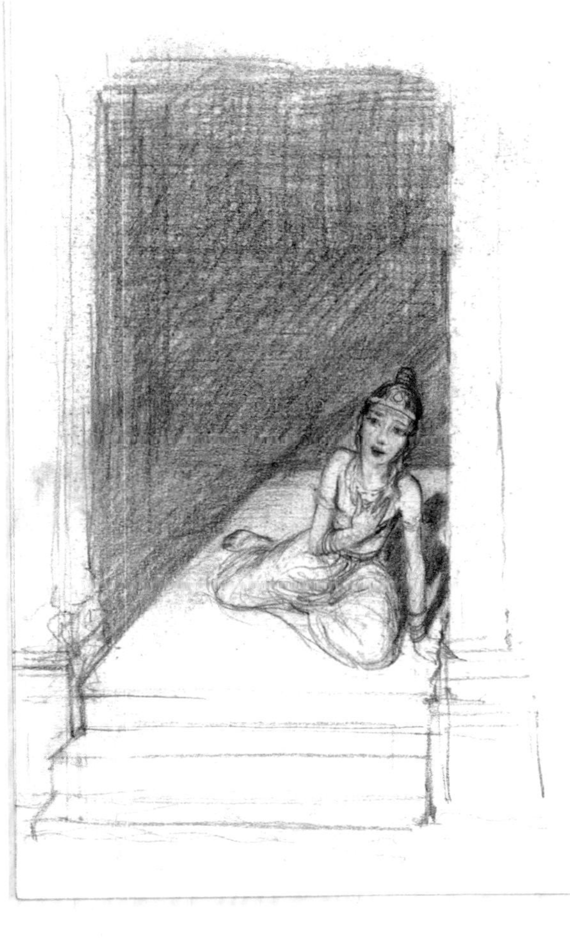

Seeing that Surya could not be swayed from his purpose, Kunti asked how she could be saved from sin.

She said, "Surely you are the very paragon of virtue upon whom the life of all beings depend. How can you therefore perform such an act?"

Surya said, "Do not fear. I would never do anything that brings suffering to another. By my power you shall remain a virgin."

Seeing that she had little choice, Kunti finally relented. By his mystic potency the god placed his energy within her, and she fell senseless onto her bed. Surya then departed, and Kunti soon realised that she was pregnant. Only she and her nurse knew, and she somehow kept her entire pregnancy hidden from everyone else in the palace. In course of time Karna was born, and the perplexed Kunti, fearing that she would lose her reputation, abandoned him soon after his birth. Placing him in a wicker basket, the tearful girl set him adrift on a nearby river, praying that his father would take care of him. She then returned sorrowfully to the palace.

Kunti and Surya
Oil on Canvas, 230 x 130 cm

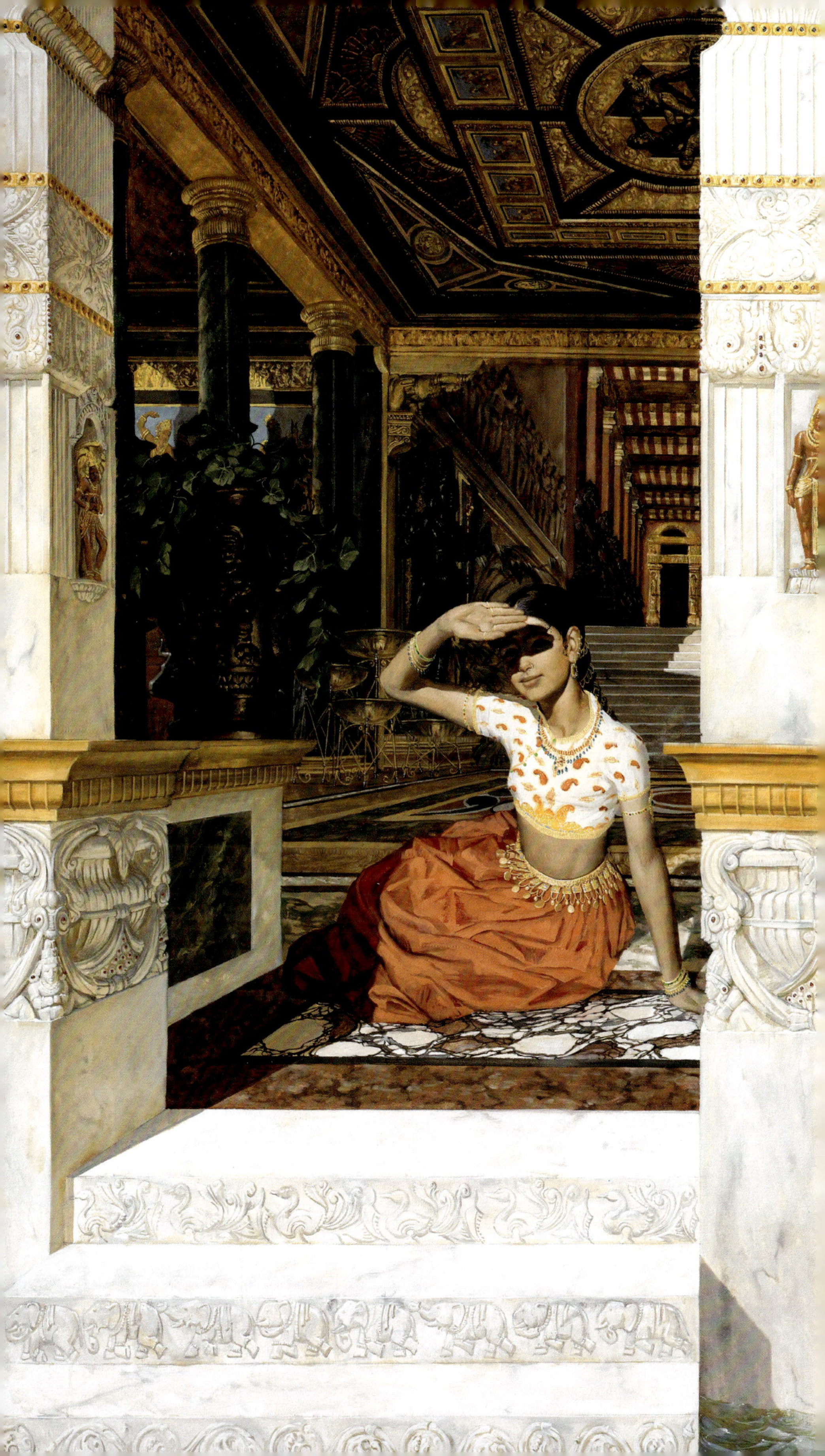

The Pandavas Enter Hastinapura

One day while hunting, King Pandu accidentally killed the sage Kindama, who was having sexual intercourse with his wife after both of them had assumed the form of deers. With his dying breath the sage cursed the king, "You also shall die like me if you ever again unite with your wife." In shock and dismay the king decided to retire to the forest, taking along his two wives, Kunti and Madri. Unable to beget children he called upon the gods to give him sons.

The great lord of religion, Dharma, united first with Kunti and begot Yudhisthira. The wind-god, Vayu, next united with her to produce Bhima. And her third son was Arjuna, from Indra, the king of the gods. Finally, the twin Ashvini gods gave Madri two sons, the twins Nakula and Sahadeva. Pandu enjoyed watching his five godly boys grow into powerful youths. He carefully avoided close contact with his wives, always remembering Kindama's thunderbolt of words.

One spring day, however, he was alone with Madri in the woods, where they had gone to gather wild fruit. Suddenly overpowered by desire he took hold of her. The horrified Madri tried to prevent him. "My lord, pray stop!" she pleaded. "Remember the curse." But Pandu could not be checked. Driven by his fate he lay with Madri in his arms, and the curse took its terrible toll. Even as Madri struggled to save her beloved husband, he fell dead in her embrace. She screamed in anguish, "No, my lord!"

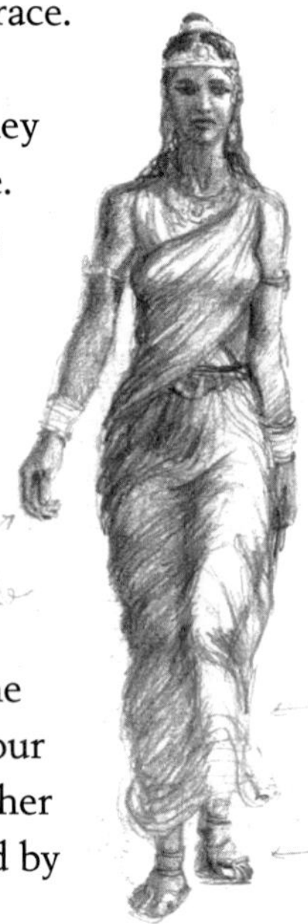

Kunti and the five boys came running. Seeing the frightful scene, they collapsed in grief. Madri was beside herself with sorrow and inconsolable. Pandu's body was taken by some forest sages and placed on a pyre, while they chanted sacred hymns. Kunti wanted to enter Pandu's funeral fire and ascend to the heavens with him, but Madri fell at her feet and begged, "Please let me go with him. Our lord approached me in love, and his desire is not yet fulfilled." The soft-hearted Kunti agreed, and Madri threw herself upon Pandu's pyre and embraced his body as the flames consumed him. She thereby followed him to his next destination.

Kunti and the five boys later sorrowfully approached the sages and asked what they should do now. The sages advised them to return to the capital, Hastinapura, at once: "The time has come for you to take your rightful place as lords of the world." The five brothers and their mother then set off for Hastinapura. They were led by the sages and accompanied by many inhabitants of the celestial region where they had been residing. Word eventually reached Hastinapura of their impending arrival, and a huge crowd gathered to greet them. Blind King Dhritarastra was led out by his brother, Vidura, and all the other Kuru elders assembled to meet Pandu's young sons for the first time.

The procession entered the city through its main gate, with the sages at its head. The Kurus immediately bowed before the learned sages and had them seated on fine rugs and seats. After they had been offered due worship, one sage said, "Know these five boys to be Pandu's sons, born from his wives by the grace of God and the demigods. Their father has ascended to heaven along with Madri, his chaste wife. His sons are now next in line for the throne. This is the truth." The sages then took their leave, and before the astonished eyes of the people they simply vanished from the spot.

Grandfather Bhishma then took the boys and their mother into the city and arranged for their accommodations in a great palace. Funeral rites were performed for Pandu, and a period of mourning was declared throughout the city for twelve days. After this the Pandavas began to live in Hastinpura, to the great envy and annoyance of Prince Duryodhana, who arrogantly considered only himself to be the rightful heir to the throne.

The Pandavas Enter Hastinapura
Oil on Canvas, 175 x 350 cm (pp. 30-31)

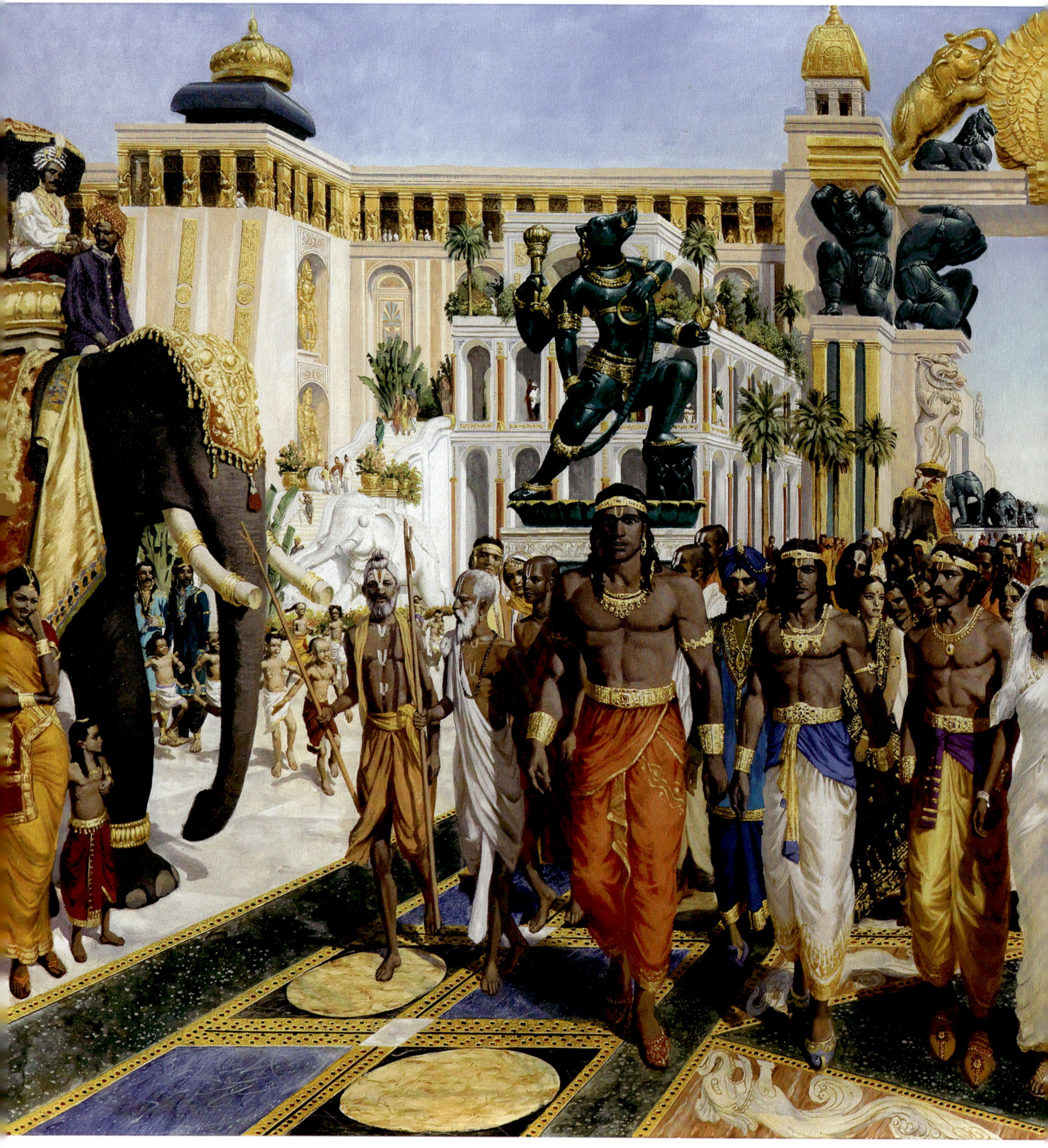

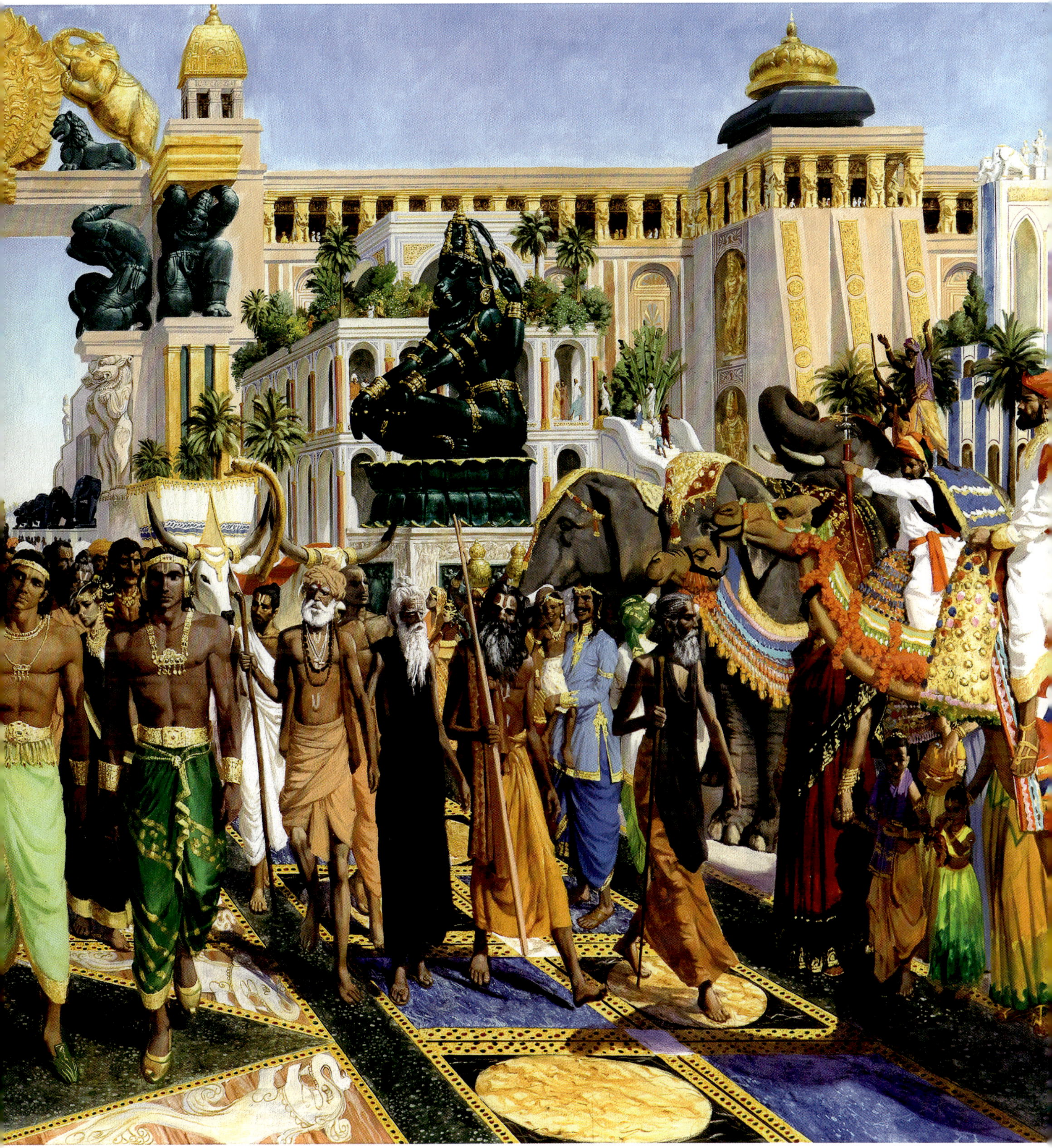

Dwaraka

Having spent several months in Indraprastha as the guest of the Pandavas, Krishna finally desired to return to his own city, Dwaraka. He had witnessed the great Rajasuya sacrifice that established Yudhisthira as the world's emperor. After spending a pleasurable time with his beloved devotees in their magnificent city, he set off for Dwaraka on his great chariot, driven by Daruka, his pure devotee and eternal charioteer.

They made good time as Daruka urged on the four celestial steeds. Passing through forests, towns, villages, and many hamlets, Krishna was greeted and worshipped with love by all who saw him.

At last they approached Dwaraka, and as they came close the Lord gave a mighty blast on his conchshell, named Panchajanya. The guards threw open the city gates, and thousands of citizens rushed out of their houses to greet Krishna. They had been longing for his return since the day of his departure, and now they lined the streets, anxious to see him again.

Krishna dismounted from his chariot and began walking on the road. The people gazed at him with unblinking eyes, drinking in his transcendental beauty. Krishna reciprocated with smiling glances and by graciously accepting their presentations of gold, cows, and valuable items. Brahmins and sages chanted prayers and praises.

Looking benevolently from side to side, Krishna moved through the city. He saw its flower gardens, orchards, lakes filled with lotuses, and delightful hermitages. Nine hundred thousand marble mansions lined its almost countless broad avenues, which were laid out symmetrically and graced by great jewelled arches. The mansions were also constructed with gold and silver, inlaid with great glittering emeralds and other precious stones.

Flags and festoons adorned the buildings, and the gateways and arches were decorated with colourful signs and garlands. Scented water was sprinkled on the spotless paved roads. Flowers, rice, and seeds were strewn everywhere. In every doorway stood auspicious items, such as fruit, sugarcane, incense, and ghee lamps and pots of yoghurt, milk, and water.

On the balconies of the buildings stood many ladies, who praised the Lord as he passed. Krishna glanced up at them, heard their praises, and threw looks of love in their direction, which made their hearts pound with excitement.

Along the delightful avenues were tall trees heavy with fruits and bright blossoms. Birds flew in and out of the branches, singing in varieties of notes, while humming bees hovered over the flowers to gather their pollen.

On the streets the citizens bustled here and there, dressed in costly garments and adorned with golden ornaments. Great elephants swayed back and forth as they walked along the roads, carrying the sophisticated city ladies who sat in their howdahs behind silk drapes.

Powerful looking warriors decked out in shining armour stood along the huge ramparts that ran around the city, their weapons at the ready. The Lord's relatives came out to greet him on golden chariots, accompanied by priests uttering sacred hymns. Musical instruments were played while dancers, dramatists, and singers depicted Krishna's pastimes.

In the sky the gods were hovering in their jewelled airplanes, along with the godly sage Narada, who sang the Lord's glories as he played his vina. Showers of flower petals rained down on Krishna's head as the heavenly music played.

Coming to the section of Dwaraka where his own palaces stood, Krishna admired its incomparable opulence. Here the celestial architect, Vishvakarma, had displayed the full extent of his divine skills. More than sixteen thousand superbly constructed palaces adorned that district. They glowed with a divine effulgence from the transcendental gems embedded in their marble walls.

The Lord continued on his way. Fanned on either side by pure white yak-tail whisks, his dark body adorned with yellow garments, Krishna walked with an infinite grace that entranced the minds of all who were fortunate enough to see him. With his dazzling beautiful features adorned with brilliant ornaments, it appeared as if the sun, moon, lightning, and rainbows simultaneously surrounded a dark cloud. The Lord then simultaneously entered his 16,108 palaces after expanding himself into that many forms.

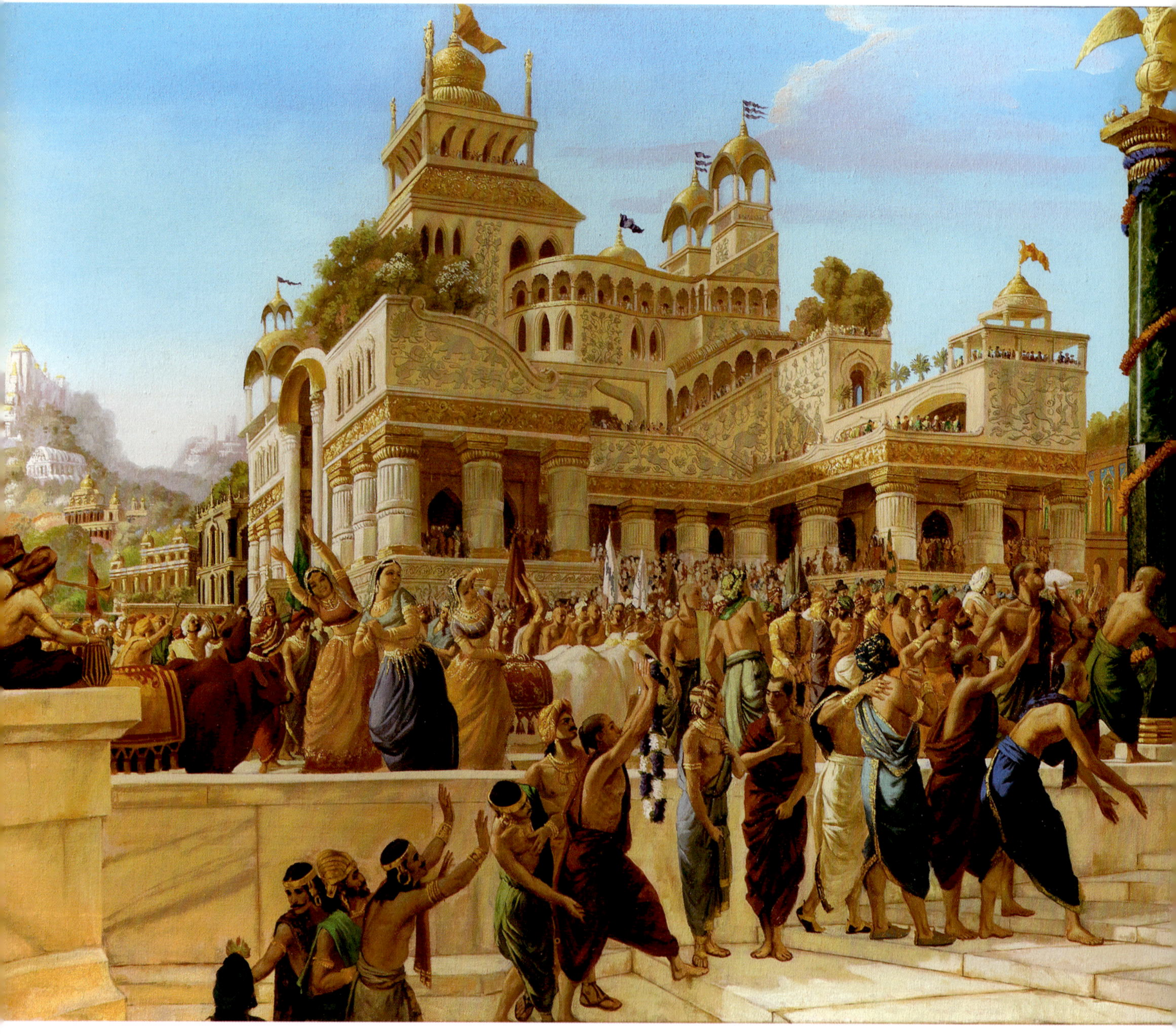

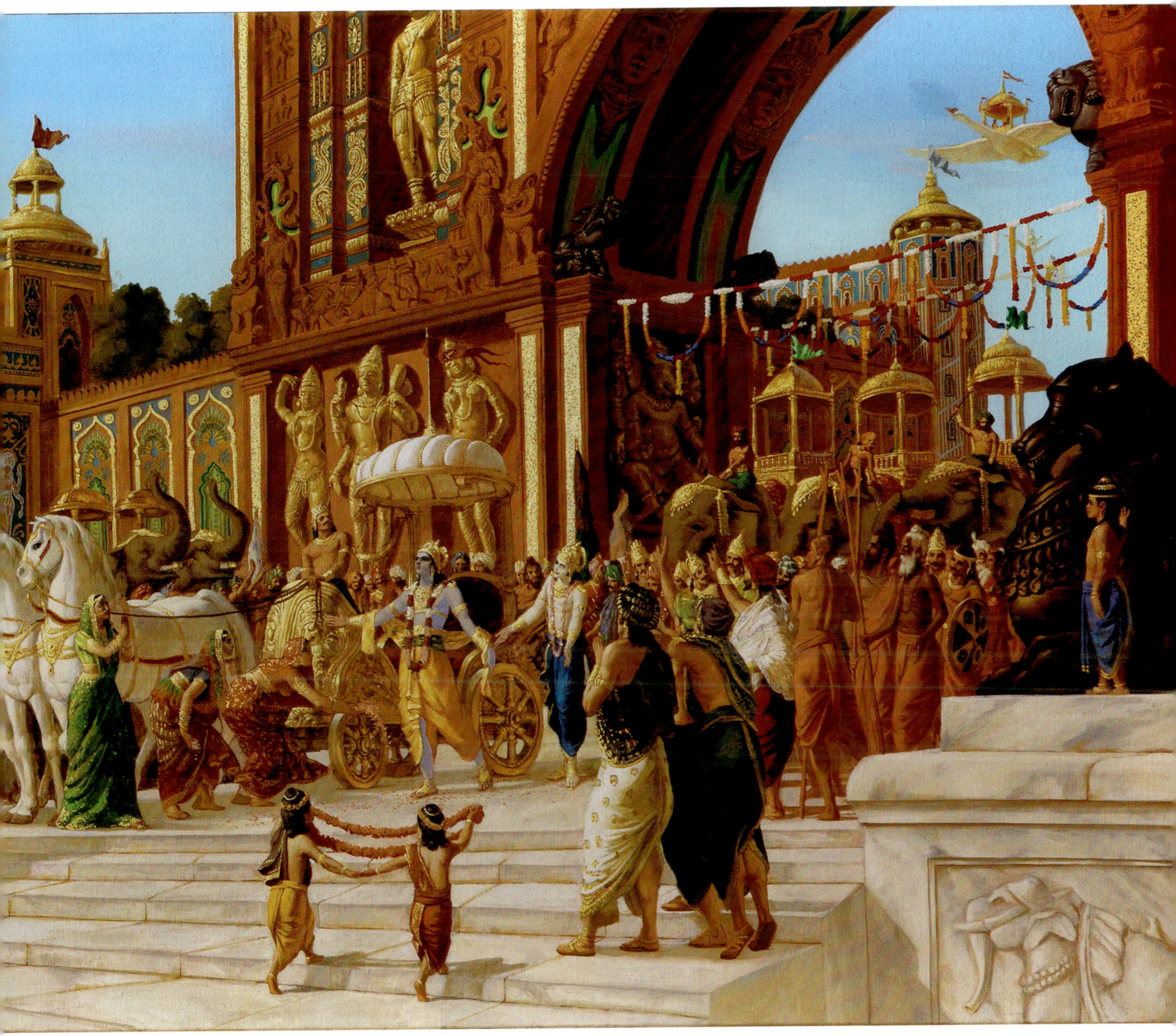

Entering Dwaraka
Oil on Canvas, 150 x 200 cm

Narada came down to one palace, where he saw Krishna and his brother, Balarama, standing on a balcony. He entered the palace and was struck by its stupendous splendour.

Supporting the palace were coral pillars, worked with vaidurya gems, which sparkled with constantly changing hues. Vishvakarma had arranged pearl-strung canopies above seats, and beds fashioned of ivory, set with precious jewels.

Many maidservants clad in costly garments, with gold necklaces around their necks, moved about the spacious rooms, their bangles and ankle bells jingling together. Gem-studded lamps brightly illuminated the long passageways, along which stood armed guards wearing turbans and jewelled earrings.

On the high roofs loudly crying peacocks danced amidst the ornate ridges, mistaking for clouds the fragrant incense smoke escaping from the latticed windows. The sage had seen the cities of the greatest gods but had never witnessed such opulence.

To his complete amazement he found that in every one of the Lord's palaces Krishna was present, acting in a different way with one of his wives. Each time the sage entered, he was lovingly welcomed by Krishna, who sat him down and bathed his feet.

After seeing how Krishna was acting exactly like a normal husband with his loving consorts, Narada left the city in astonishment, constantly singing his glories.

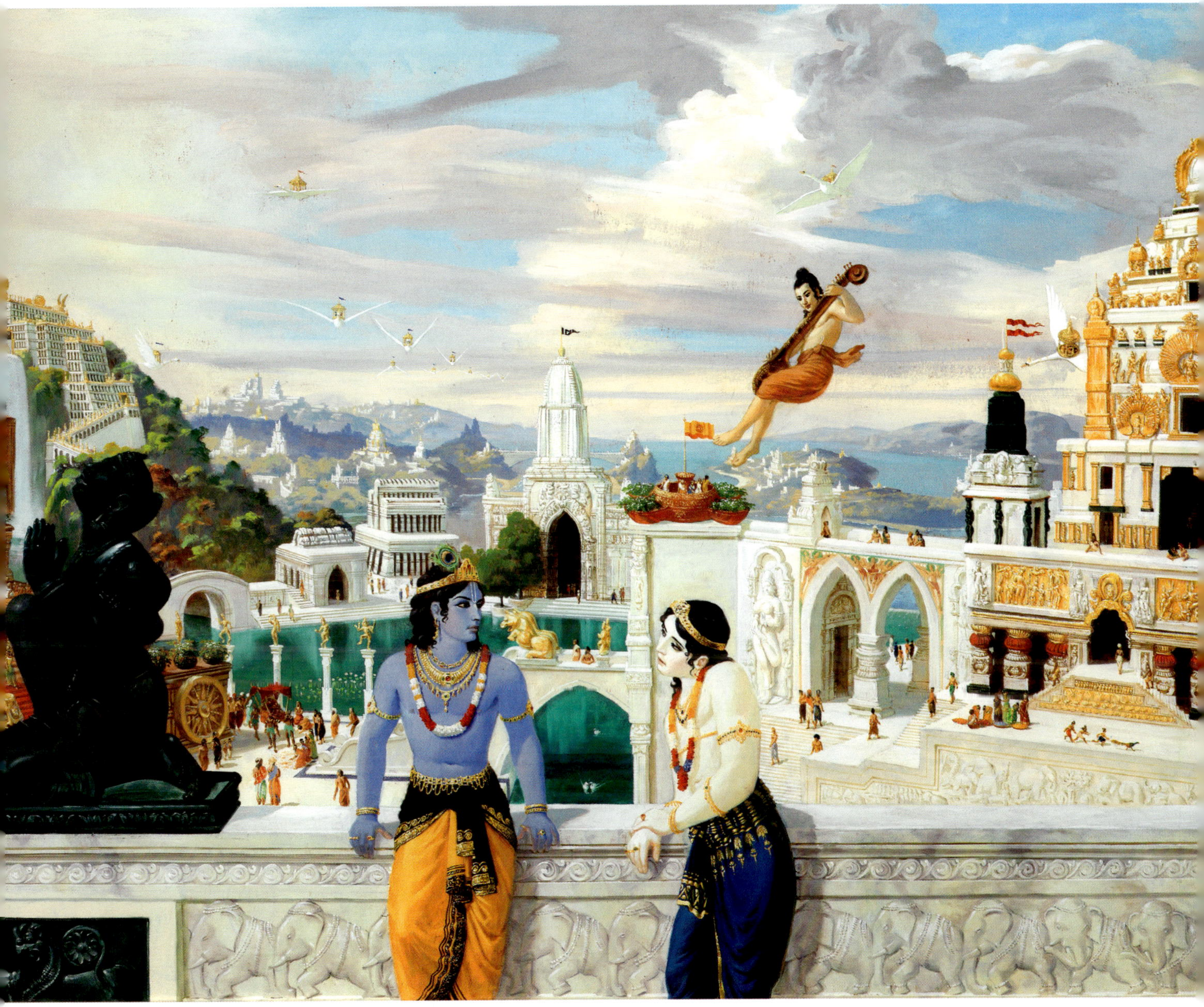

My Dwaraka
Oil on Canvas, 150 x 200 cm

The Demoness Hidimbi

At the behest of the blind King Dhritarastra, the Pandavas and their mother went for a vacation to the city of Varanavata. There an attempt was made by the king's oldest son, Duryodhana, to kill them in a great house fire, but they had escaped beforehand. Fleeing from the city, the young princes and their mother fearfully struggled through a dense forest. As they went deeper and deeper into the wilds the strongest of them, Bhima, lifted them all onto his mighty frame and carried them.

Arriving at a clearing, they stopped to rest, and the exhausted brothers and their mother fell into a deep sleep. Only Bhima stayed awake, vigilantly guarding them from all danger. Not far from where Bhima sat there lived a terrible Rakshasa named Hidimba, along with his sister, Hidimbi.

The demon immediately detected the presence of the some human beings, and he said to his sister, "My dear Hidimbi, can you smell the humans? Long has it been since we tasted their flesh. Surely they are not far from here. Go quickly and find them. Let us feast upon their bodies and quaff their foaming blood."

Hidimbi cackled in glee. She shook her long orange hair and opened her blood red eyes. Extending her claws, she dropped down from a tree and went swiftly and silently through the trees towards the scent. When she reached the clearing where the brothers lay, she stopped and peered out from behind the trunk of a huge tree. She saw Bhima seated at ease near his sleeping mother and brothers.

Hidimbi gazed at the powerful prince. He resembled a god. His skin was golden, his well-muscled frame was dark and lithe, his face aquiline, adorned with black curls, and his copper coloured eyes were like lotus petals.

The Rakshasi was struck by the arrows of desire. She had to have this splendid man as her husband. In an instant she exercised her mystical power and transformed herself into a beautiful girl dressed in fine silks and adorned with celestial ornaments.

She walked slowly toward Bhima, glancing down bashfully and then said, "Great hero, who are you? What are you doing in these woods?"

Bhima looked at her in wonder. How did such a delicate looking woman find her way into such a deep and dangerous forest?

Detecting his thoughts, Hidimbi smiled and said, "Know me to be Hidimbi, sister of Hidimba who has asked me to bring you back for his meal."

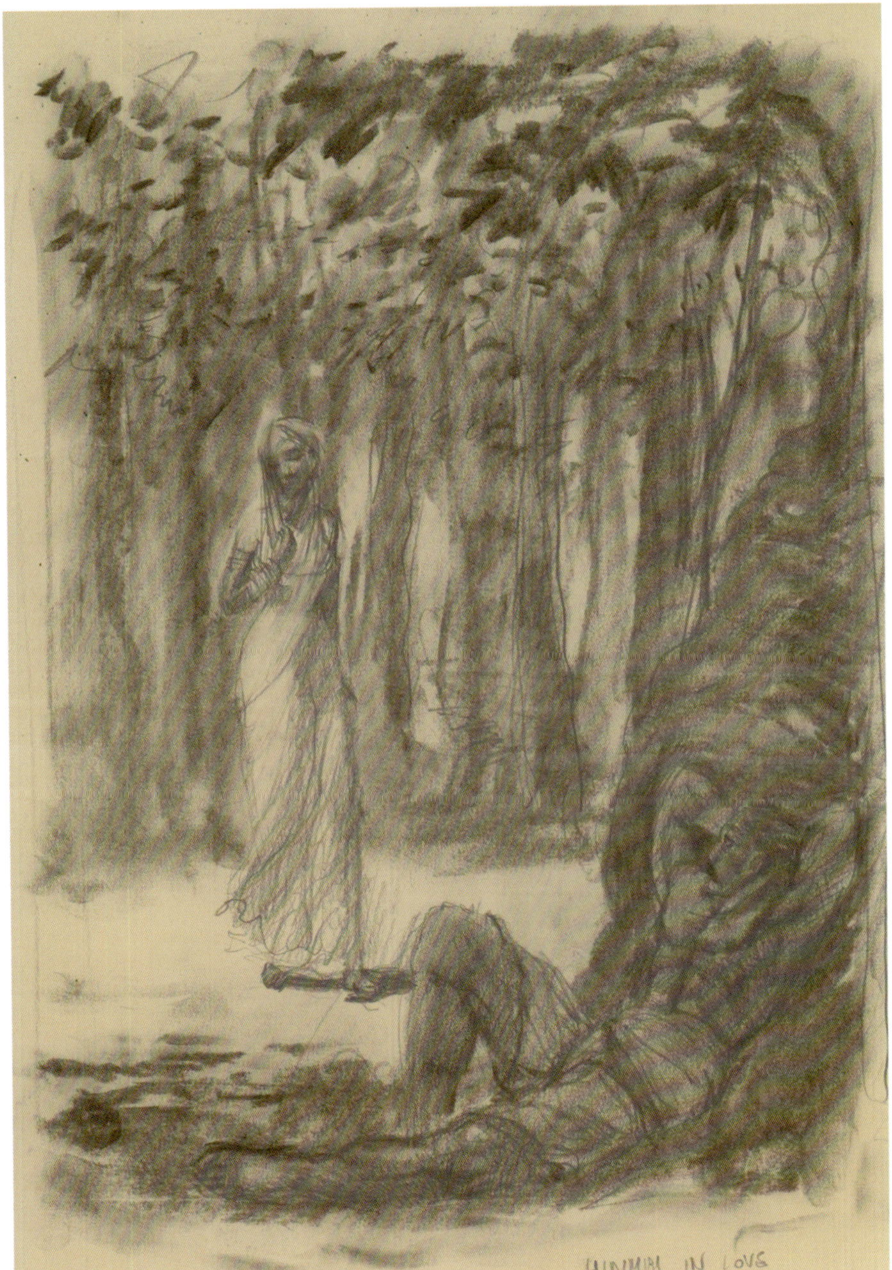
HIDIMBI IN LOVE

Bhima leapt up, but the Rakshasi reassured him that she would not try to harm him: "Indeed, I now desire you as my husband. Let us leave together at once and enjoy as man and wife. I will carry you to celestial gardens high in the mountains where the gods and their consorts sport together."

Hidimbi smiled alluringly, but Bhima, unmoved, gave a short laugh and said, "How could I leave my mother and brothers simply to satisfy my lust? Go, stay or bring your demon-brother here. I care not."

Hidimbi implored him not to waste any time: "Come with me now while you still can. You will not survive an encounter with my brother. Many times have I seen him slay humans."

Bhima looked at her and said nothing. He was not going anywhere. By this time Hidimba had decided to find out for himself what was happening.

When Hidimba arrived at the clearing and saw his transformed sister talking to Bhima, he roared in fury with a voice like thunder and then said to her, "How dare you disregard me! You have dishonoured the Rakshasa race by offering yourself to a human. I shall kill you first and then these take care of these others."

He rushed at Hidimbi, but Bhima stepped in front of him and said, "You shall not harm a woman in my sight. See now my power. I shall tear you to pieces."

A great fight then took place between them, which knocked down all the trees in that region. As his mother and brothers looked on in awe, Bhima slew the huge demon, pounding him to a pulp. After this, on the instructions of his brother Yudhisthira, he accepted Hidimbi as his wife. By him she gave birth to Ghatotkacha, the mighty Rakshsa warrior who would play a significant part in the great war to follow.

The Demoness Hidimbi
Oil on Canvas, 130 x 90 cm

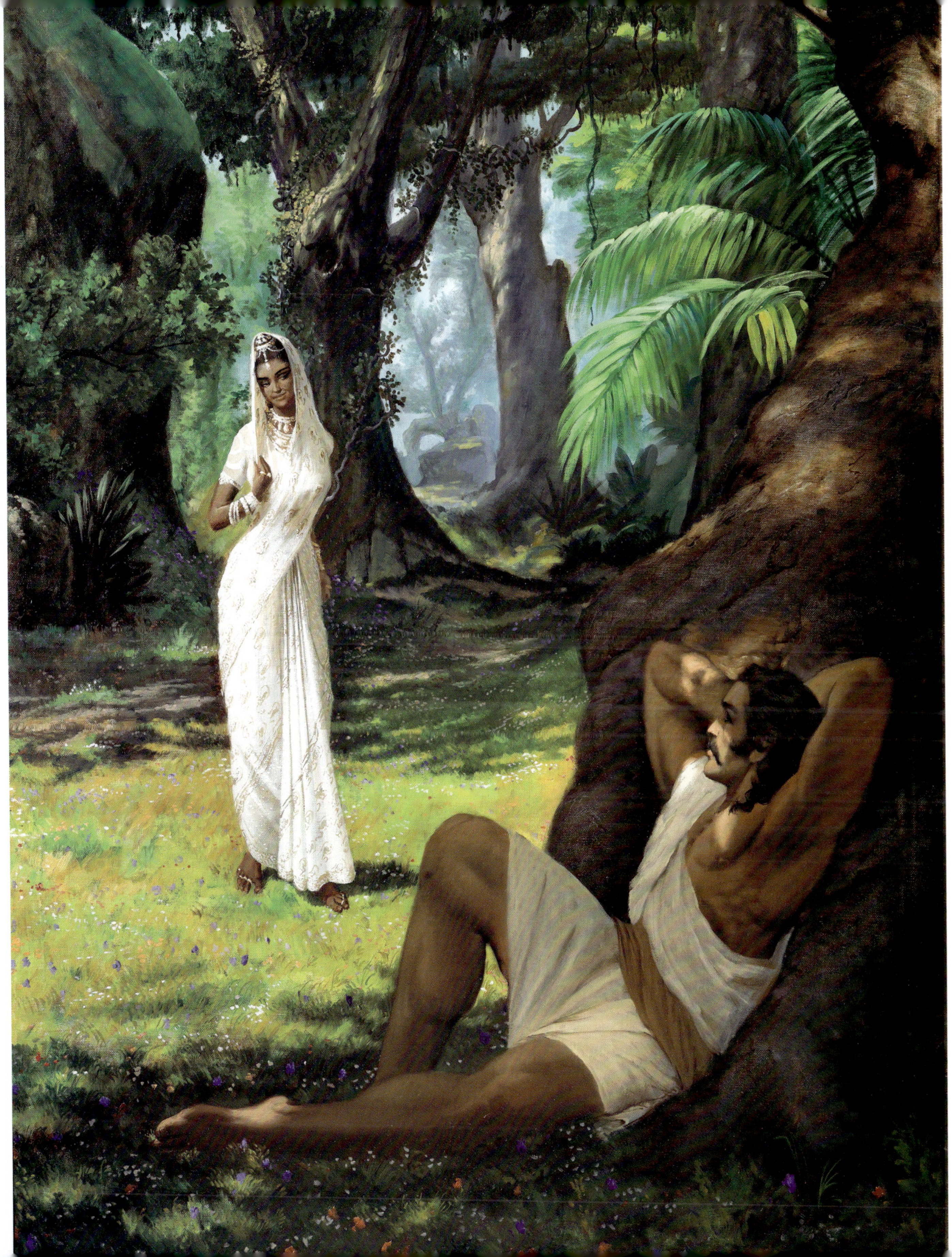

Kunti and Draupadi

Arjuna raised the great bow that so many kings had not even been able to string. He drew the arrow back to his ear and took careful aim. A powerful crack rang out around the arena as shot the arrow. It streaked upwards and struck the target cleanly in the middle, bringing it down with a crash. The crowd sent up a great cheer as Arjuna turned towards the royal dais where Draupadi stood, now holding the nuptial garland. Moving gracefully, she came down with her brother, Dhristadyumna, and placed it around Arjuna's neck. He had succeeded where all other young royals had failed, in winning the princess's hand in the great challenge of archery skill set by her father, King Drupada.

Other than Krishna and Balarama, no one else knew that it was Arjuna who had hit the target. Having recently escaped an attempt to murder them, the Pandavas were disguised as Brahmins. Everyone in the assembly was amazed to see a young Brahmin so skilled at archery, but the visiting royalty present was not impressed. How could Drupada allow his beautiful daughter to wed a poor Brahmin, leaving aside all the world's great princes and kings? Intending to punish him, they rose up and advanced on Drupada with weapons raised. Still holding the bow, Arjuna ran to his assistance with Bhima by his side. Drupada was now as good as his father.

Heading the opposing side was Karna, who declared, "Brahmins should not be attacked, but if they stand ready for battle then they may be fought."

This was met with a cheer of approval from the others. Karna immediately fired a volley of arrows at Arjuna, who warded them off with just his bow. Swiftly taking up the arrows meant for the challenge, he fought back as Bhima tore up a great tree and rushed at the attacking kings. The two heroes held them off as their three brothers slipped away with Draupadi, back toward the potter's hut where they were residing. The fighting went on for some minutes, with Arjuna beating back

Karna, and Bhima overpowering another powerful foe named Shalya in hand-to-hand combat. Finally

Krishna, who had been observing everything from the stands, came forward and spoke.

"In my view the maiden has been fairly and wonderfully won by this Brahmin. We do not need to spoil the occasion with bloodshed. Let him go with his prize."

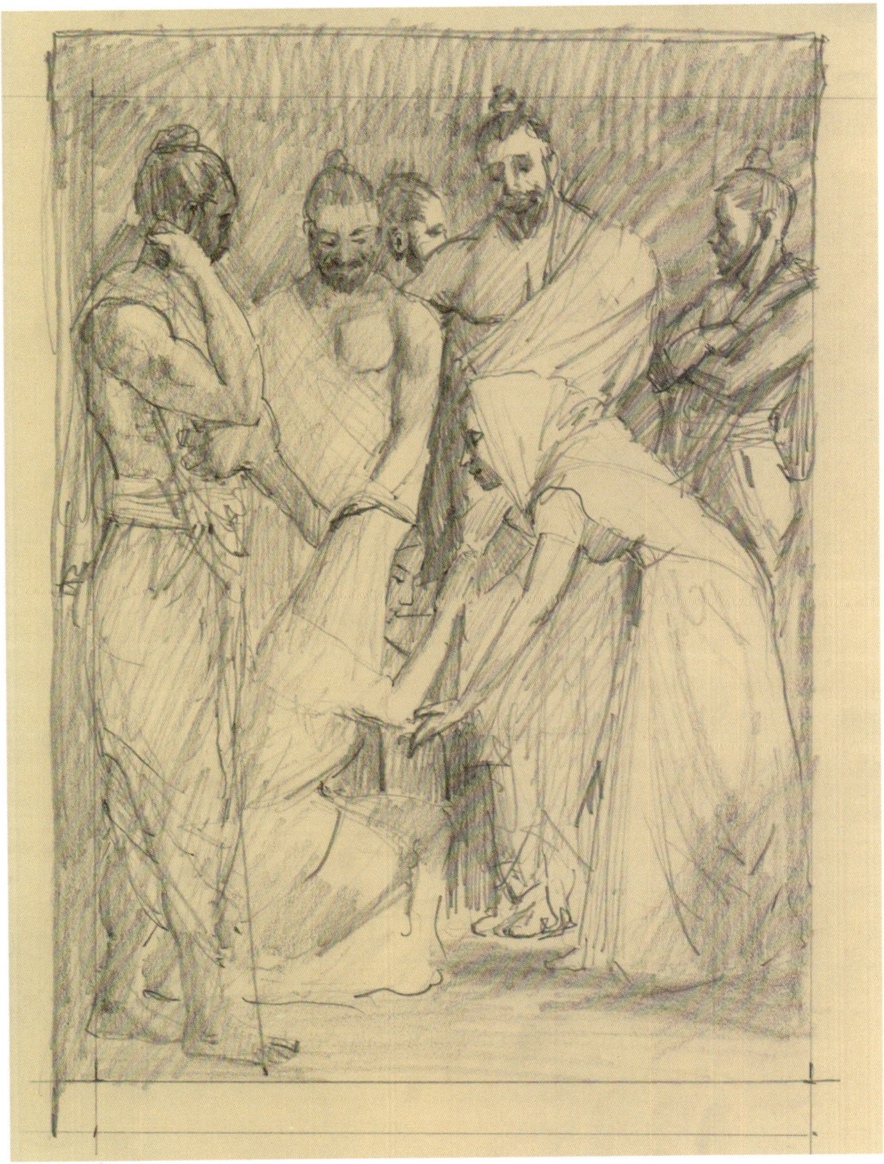

Having realised that the two brothers could not be easily overcome, the disappointed rivals reluctantly agreed. They lowered their weapons and slowly dispersed as Arjuna and Bhima left the arena surrounded by clamouring Brahmins. They came out of the great stadium like the sun and moon emerging from behind clouds and soon caught up to their brothers, who were waiting with Draupadi. They then returned to the hut where their mother, Kunti, was anxiously awaiting them.

As they entered the hut Arjuna, looking at Draupadi, called out, "Mother, just see the wonderful alms we have obtained today."

Disguised as Brahmins they had daily begged for their food, and when they brought it back their mother would share it out among them.

Thinking that they had again brought food, she responded, "Let it be shared among you all."

She came out of the room where she had been sitting with a smile on her face, but when she saw Draupadi, her expression changed.

"What have I said?" she exclaimed. "How can you all share this maiden?"

Seeing Queen Kunti before her, Draupadi bowed at her feet. Kunti's heart melted to see her humility, and she blessed her by saying, "Gentle girl, you shall be the wife of heroes and the mother of heroes."

Turning to Yudhisthira she said, "What can be done now? I have never spoken an untruth, but how can my words prove true in this case?"

Yudhisthira was thoughtful. Looking at his brothers, who were repeatedly glancing at Draupadi, he finally said, "This princess shall become the wife of us all. Surely it is the arrangement of providence."

The brothers all looked at the lovely Draupadi. As always, Yudhisthira had found the perfect solution.

Kunti and Draupadi
Oil on Canvas, 160 x 120 cm

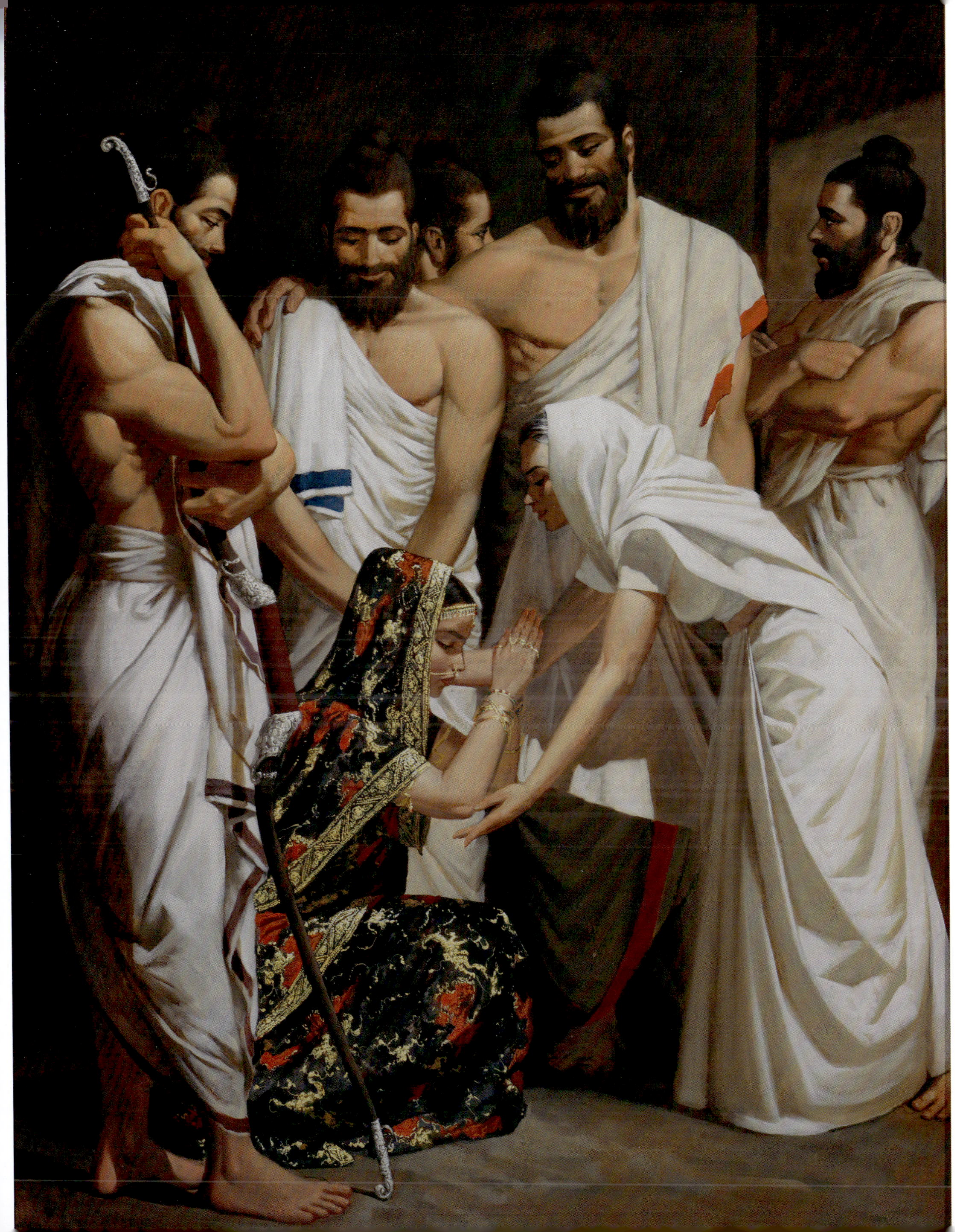

Krishna in Indraprastha

After their plan to kill the Pandavas in a house fire had failed, the Kauravas consulted together. The five brothers had emerged from hiding and were now staying in Drupada's palace. Arjuna had won the hand of the king's beautiful daughter, Draupadi, in the great archery challenge.

As the Kauravas met in their assembly hall, Karna expressed his view that they should immediately attack: "While the Pandavas are yet not strong let us take our forces to Drupada's capital and crush them at once."

His proposal met with the approval of Duryodhana and his brothers, but some Kuru elders such as Bhishma, Drona, and Vidura counselled against such an idea.

"The only right course of action is to give them half the kingdom," said Bhishma.

Finally, King Dhritarastra, although inclined to his own sons, relented and told Vidura to go to the Pandavas and bring them back to Hastinapura: "It is our good fortune that they survived the great fire in Varanavata and that they have obtained the celestial Draupadi as their wife. Bring them here in peace and let us enjoy their company again."

When the brothers returned with Draupadi, the people of Hastinapura were overjoyed. It had been thought that they perished in the burning house, and it now seemed as if they had returned from the dead. The citizens spilled onto the streets to catch a glimpse of the Pandavas and exclaimed, "How fortunate! It is as if King Pandu has returned."

The people also feasted their eyes on the beauty of Krishna, who accompanied the Pandavas. The procession appeared like the gods entering Indra's capital, Amaravati. They were received by Bhishma and other elders and shown into the palace.

Dhritarastra then called an assembly in the great council chamber and said, "So that there shall be no further disputes let the kingdom be divided in two. I therefore award the region of Khandava to the Pandavas. Dear boys, go there and live peacefully."

Krishna smiled. This was indeed half the kingdom, but it was a desert. Long ago a Kuru king had offended a sage, who had then placed a curse upon the land that it would remain barren. Krishna looked at Yudhisthira to see how he reacted. The guileless Pandava simply folded his palms and thanked the king by saying, "It shall be as you say."

The next day the five brothers went with Krishna to the region and began to plan a city. Vyasadeva appeared there and performed sacred rituals to sanctify the land. After this, Krishna summoned Indra. When the god appeared, he bowed before Krishna and asked for his instruction. Krishna said, "Sprinkle your heavenly nectar across this land to counter the effects of the curse upon it. Then construct a city to rival those of the gods."

Indra immediately did as he was asked and called for Vishvakarma, the celestial architect, who set about building a magnificent city. Granite walls rose to the skies all around the perimeter of the site, and within them numerous white marble mansions and palaces were constructed. Broad highways of red stone stretched in all directions. The land contained spacious gardens and orchards with clear lakes crowded with swans. Many fine temples were built with shining golden turrets and domes. The city appeared no less splendid than Amaravati.

When it was complete, the Pandavas stood on the balcony of their palace with Krishna, who said to Yudhisthira, "This fine city will spread your name and fame."

Many men of all orders of life joyfully came there to live under the righteous rule of the Pandavas, and the city became opulent in every respect. Krishna remained with the Pandavas for several months and then returned to Dwaraka.

Krishna in Indraprastha
Oil on Canvas, 200 x 250 cm (pp. 48-49)

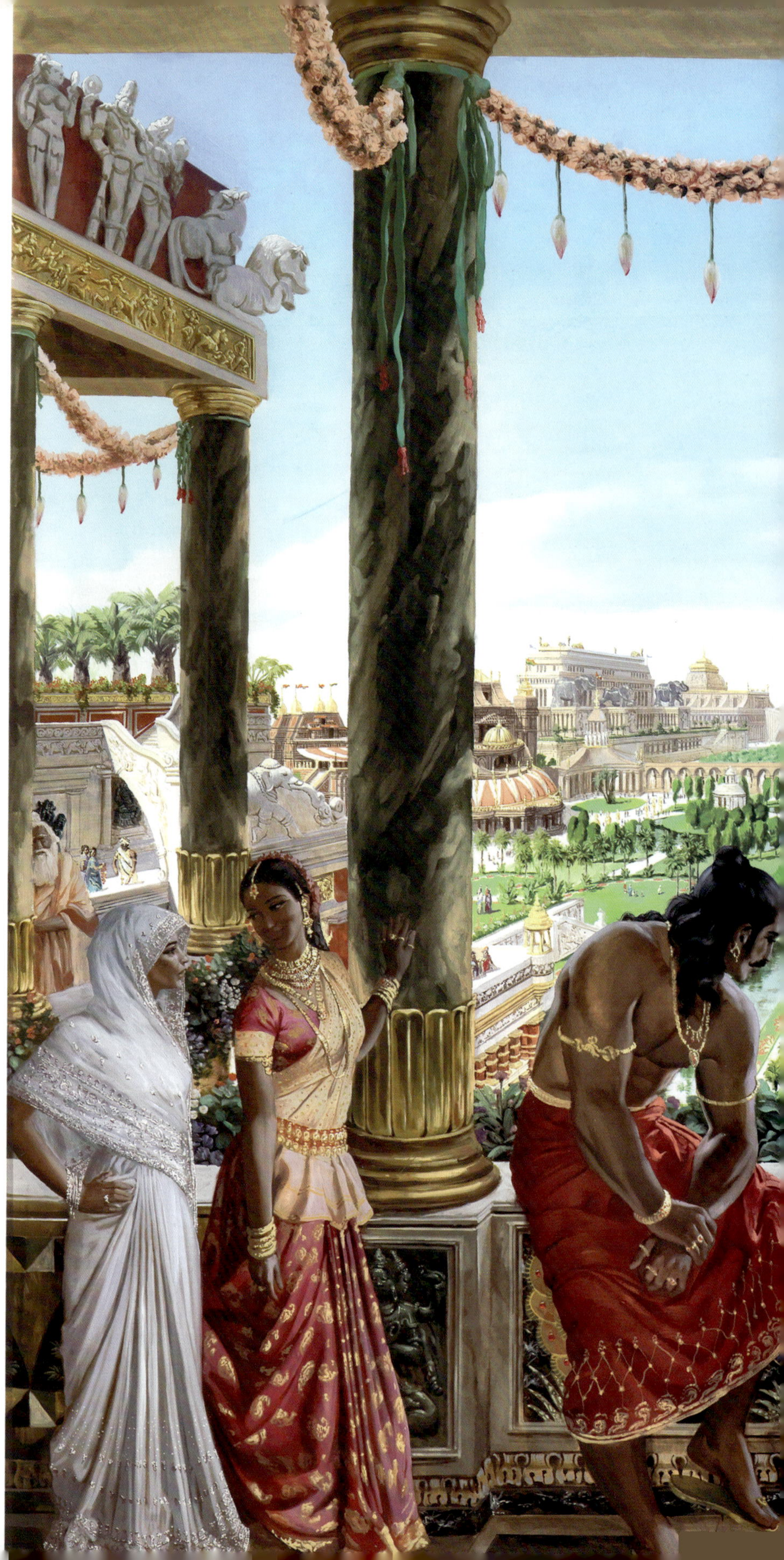

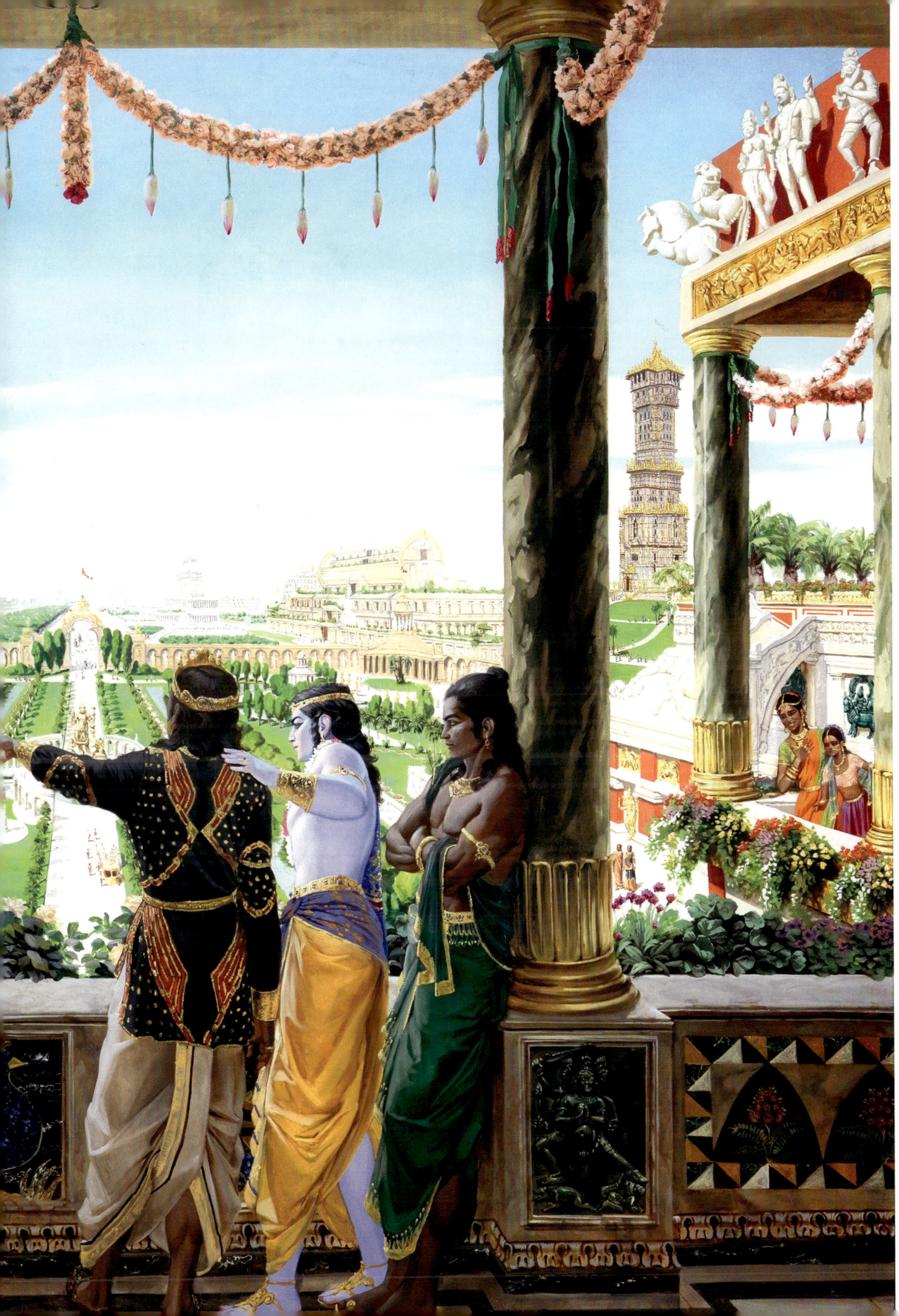

Towards Badarika-ashram

Arjuna had been in the heavens for almost five years. Soon he would return. The sage Lomasha told the other Pandavas that they should meet Arjuna as he descended from heaven onto the summit of the Gandhamadana mountain. They decided to go there to await Arjuna's arrival.

The path to the mountain peak, however, was fraught with danger. So Lomasha asked Yudhisthira to tell his servants and most of the Brahmins to stay back, because the journey would prove too difficult for them.

Then Bhima placed Draupadi on his shoulders, and the party, with only a few Brahmins, made its way along a few craggy mountain paths into the Himalayan range. The terrain was rugged; the climb arduous.

At last they came to the Alakananda river, said to descend to earth from the heavens. They worshipped the holy river and bathed in its crystal waters.

The brothers looked around at the brilliant scenery surrounding them on a high mountain plateau. It seemed as though they had arrived on a heavenly planet. Blossoming trees of every colour gave off celestial fragrances. The ground was carpeted with soft bluish grasses and expanses of wild flowers. Transparent lakes filled with blue lotuses and crowded with swans and other birds lay amid groves of fruit trees. The musical sounds of cuckoos, peacocks and countless other birds filled the air. Lomasha told the Pandavas that the king of the gods, Indra, came daily to this region to perform rituals and offer prayers.

The brothers saw in the distance what appeared to be a number of massive white mountains, but Lomasha told them that these were the bones of Naraka, a mighty demon slain by Lord Vishnu in a past age. The sage related the story as they travelled onward toward Gandhamadana.

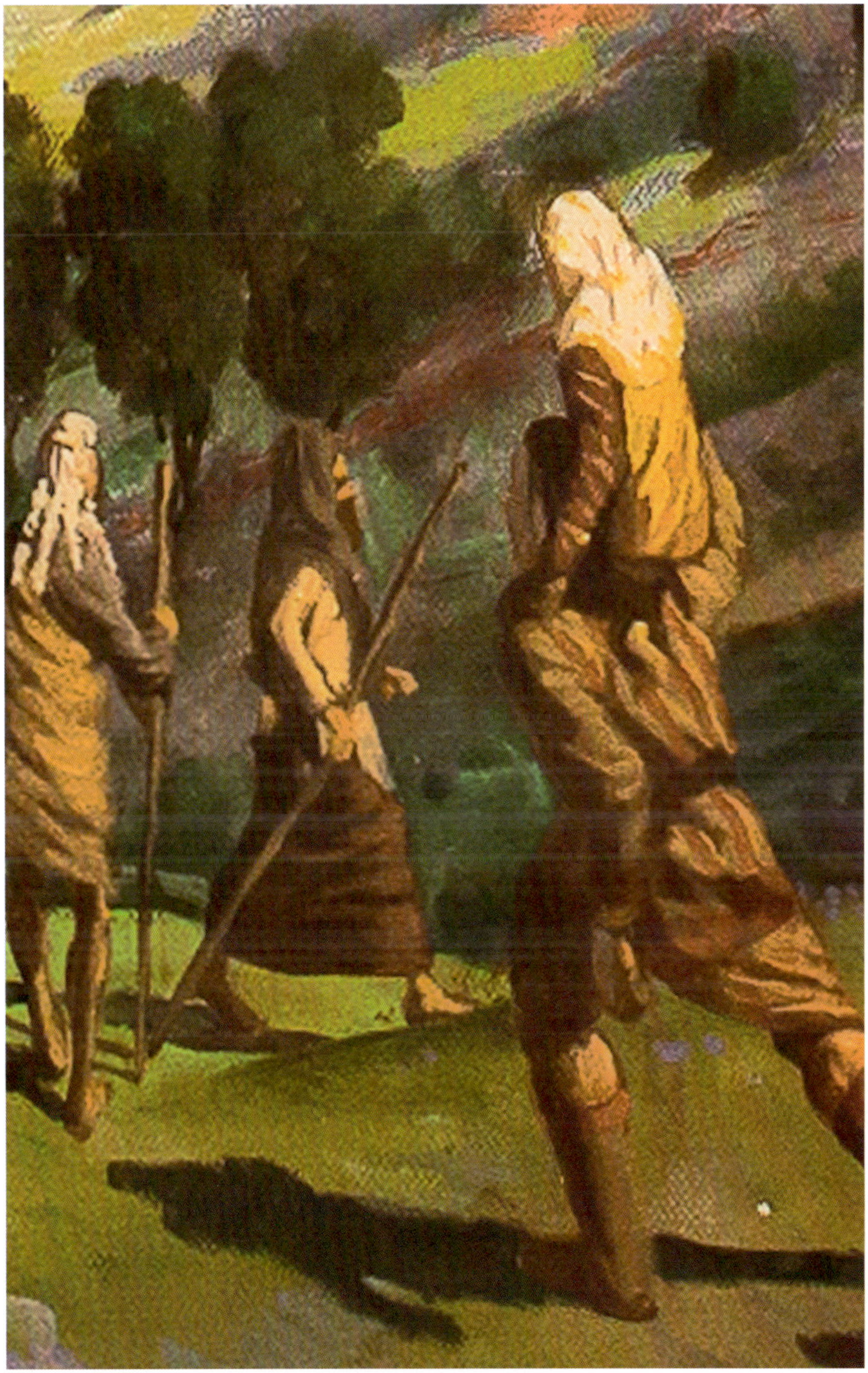

As they approached the mountain, the path became increasingly difficult. Leaving behind the heavenly terrain, they moved slowly along snow-bound and rocky paths.

Suddenly, a violent wind blew up and filled the air with dust and dried leaves, which blinded the Pandavas. Bhima held onto Draupadi, who became terror stricken as she heard trees crash to the ground around them. It almost felt like the mountain itself was being torn asunder by a celestial power.

Each of them sought whatever shelter they could find beneath rocks or some huge trees. When the dust storm subsided, rain fell in torrents. Rivulets and streams began flowing everywhere, covered in froth and mud. As the rain continued, the streams grew louder and wider, carrying away bushes. The sky was thick with black clouds throwing out lightning that seemed to play with grace upon the mountainsides.

Gradually the storm abated and the sky cleared. The sun shone brightly and steam began to rise from the ground.

The travellers emerged from their secure places and reunited, then continued toward Gandhamadana, their minds set upon seeing their beloved Arjuna again.

Towards Badarika-ashram
Oil on Canvas, 100 x 70 cm

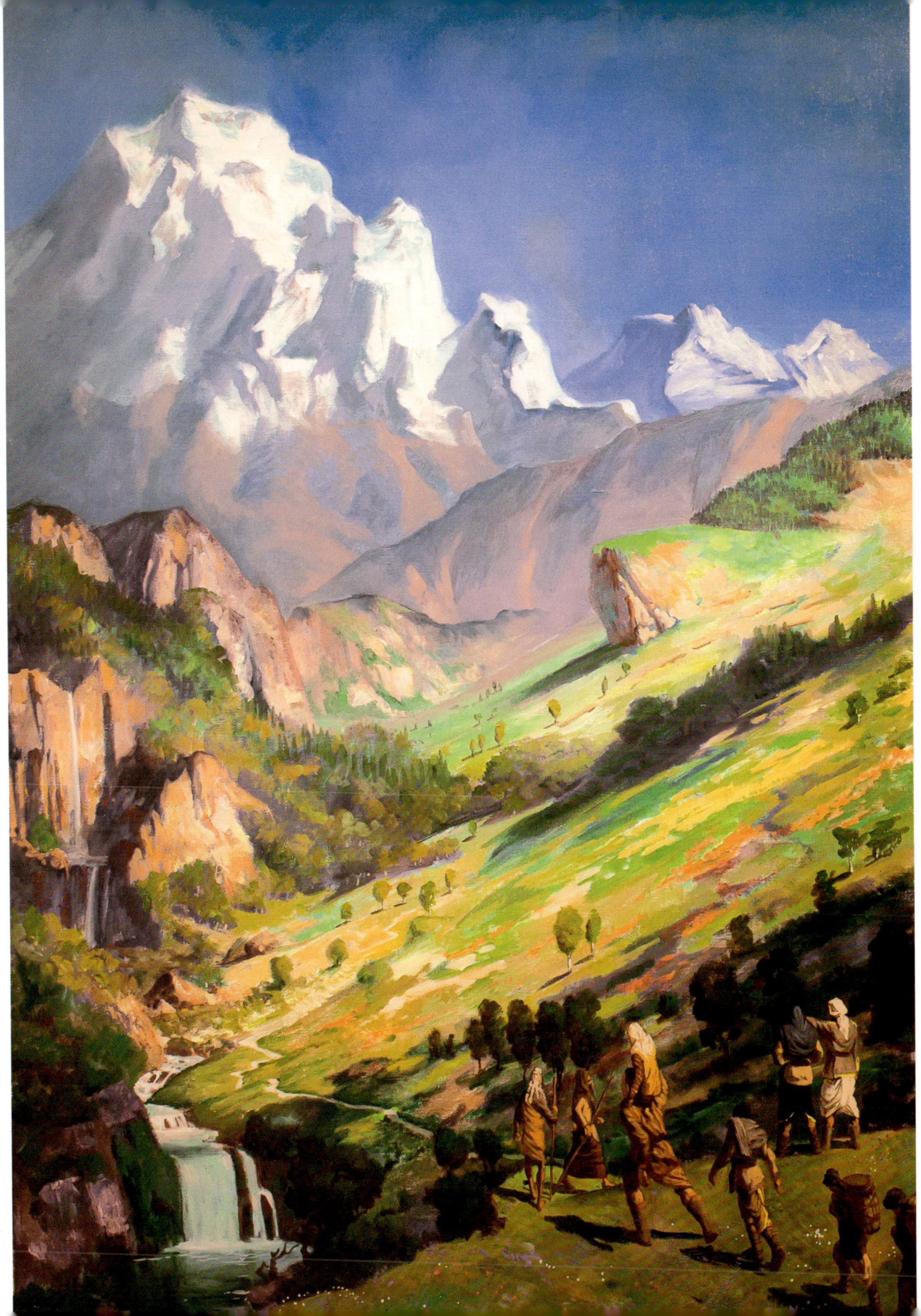

Sishupala Insults Krishna

Having become settled in their capital city, Indraprastha, the Pandavas set about performing the great Rajasuya sacrifice. This would establish Yudhisthira as the world's emperor, but that was not the reason why he wished to perform the ritual. His only desire was to glorify Krishna, his beloved Lord. He knew that all the great demigods, sages, and kings would attend and thus be in Krishna's presence. And if Krishna was worshipped as the foremost person amongst them all, this would demonstrate to the world his true, supreme position.

With this in mind the king set about making preparations. He dispatched his four brothers in the four directions, to secure the agreement of all other monarchs, either peaceably or, if necessary, after a fight. When he had gained the acquiescence of all kings, he arranged for the sacrifice itself. Kings and princes came to Indraprastha from everywhere. A great arena had been built, and they all took their places on exalted, jewelled seats. From the heavens the demigods descended, headed by Brahma, along with many celestials. All the very important persons in the universe attended.

The six sacred fires were kindled and offerings made to satisfy Vishnu and the gods. When the rituals were complete, it was time to worship the important personalities present in the assembly. The priests prepared an offering with extracts from the soma plant and other sanctified substances. Now was time for Yudhisthira to select the person he considered the foremost personality among all those present. Yudhisthira wanted to worship Krishna, but not wanting to make a unilateral decision he turned to his counsellors and asked them for advice. There was no clear consensus, so the king asked Bhishma for his opinion.

Bhishma said, "Even as the sun shines forth amidst all other luminaries, so does Krishna shine forth amidst those at this assembly. He should receive the first offering without any doubt." Yudhisthira immediately agreed and asked Sahadeva to stand and announce his intentions. Sahadeva proclaimed, "The king will now offer the first worship to Krishna. No one should object for Krishna is the Supreme Absolute Truth, the goal of perfected yogis and the Supersoul of all beings. By satisfying him we will satisfy the entire creation."

A great cheer went up from the assembly, including from the gods, sages, and other celestials. But there were a few kings who did not agree. Shishupala in particular hated Krishna, having seen Krishna carry away his intended wife, Rukmini. He leapt to his feet and began to object in angry tones: "Krishna is simply a cowherd from a village, and here we have so many great sages and gods. It is absurd to worship him first. It is like giving a sacrificial offering to a dog rather than the gods."

Shishupala continued to rail against Krishna. Many in the assembly, including the Pandavas, wanted to stop him, but Bhishma checked them and explained that Krishna would deal with Shishupala in his own time. Krishna had formerly promised Shishupala's mother that he would tolerate a hundred insults from Shishupala before taking any action. He therefore sat patiently as Shishupala spat out his furious offenses.

At the hundredth insult, Krishna challenged him: "You wretch! You have committed many sinful acts, including murder, kidnapping, rape and plunder. Your time has now come. I shall slay you before this very assembly."

Shishupala had been about to leave in disgust, but upon hearing Krishna's challenge he turned to face him and reached for his sword. Without a moment's delay Krishna raised his invincible chakra weapon, and it flew from his hand towards Shishupala, whose earrings glittered in the sunshine. It instantly severed his head, which fell to the ground. Before everyone's eyes, a brilliant spiritual spark left Shishupala's body and merged with Krishna. Gradually the assembly settled down, and after the dead body had been removed, the worship of Krishna was duly performed.

Sishupala Insults Krishna
Oil on Canvas, 150 x 200 cm (pp. 56-57)

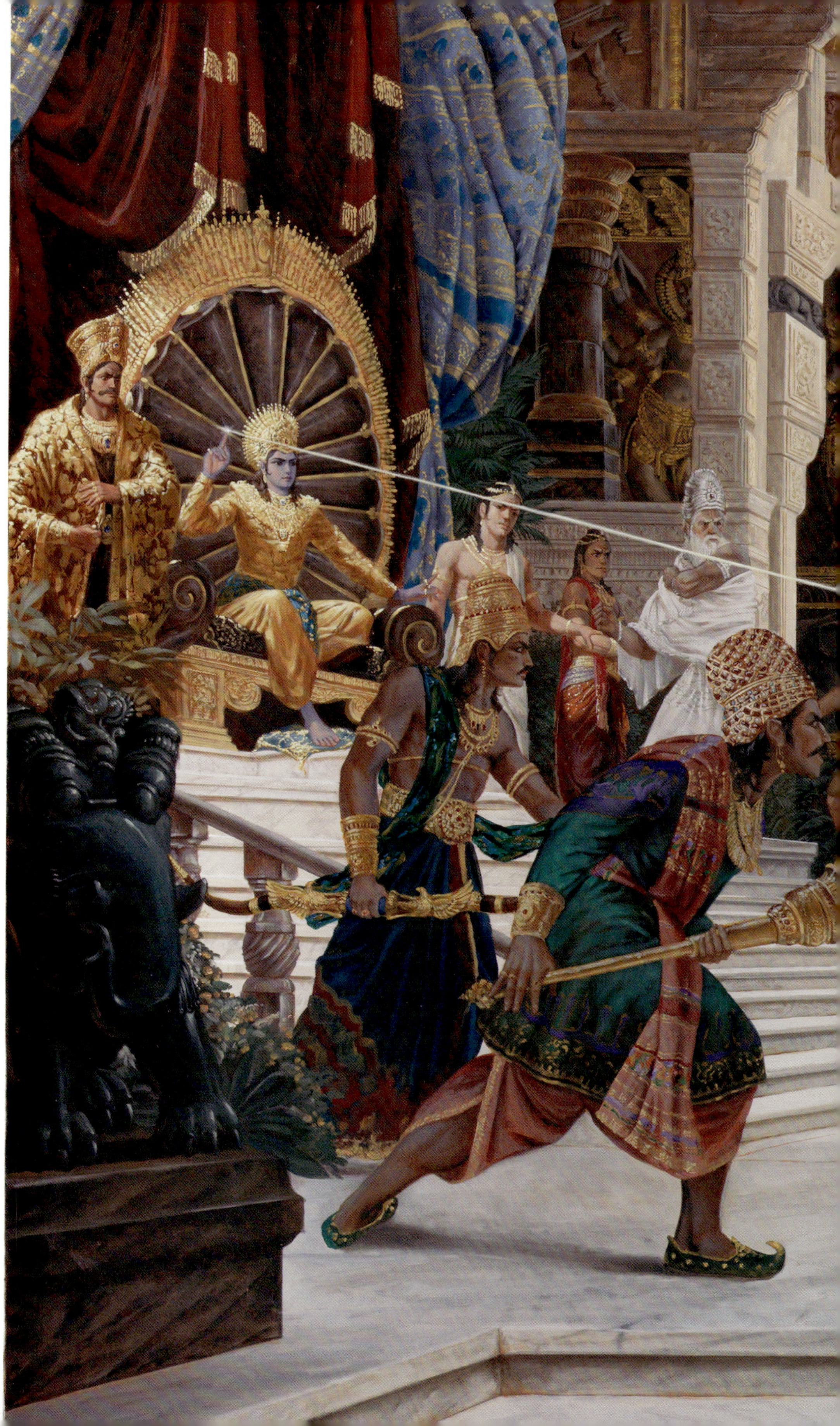

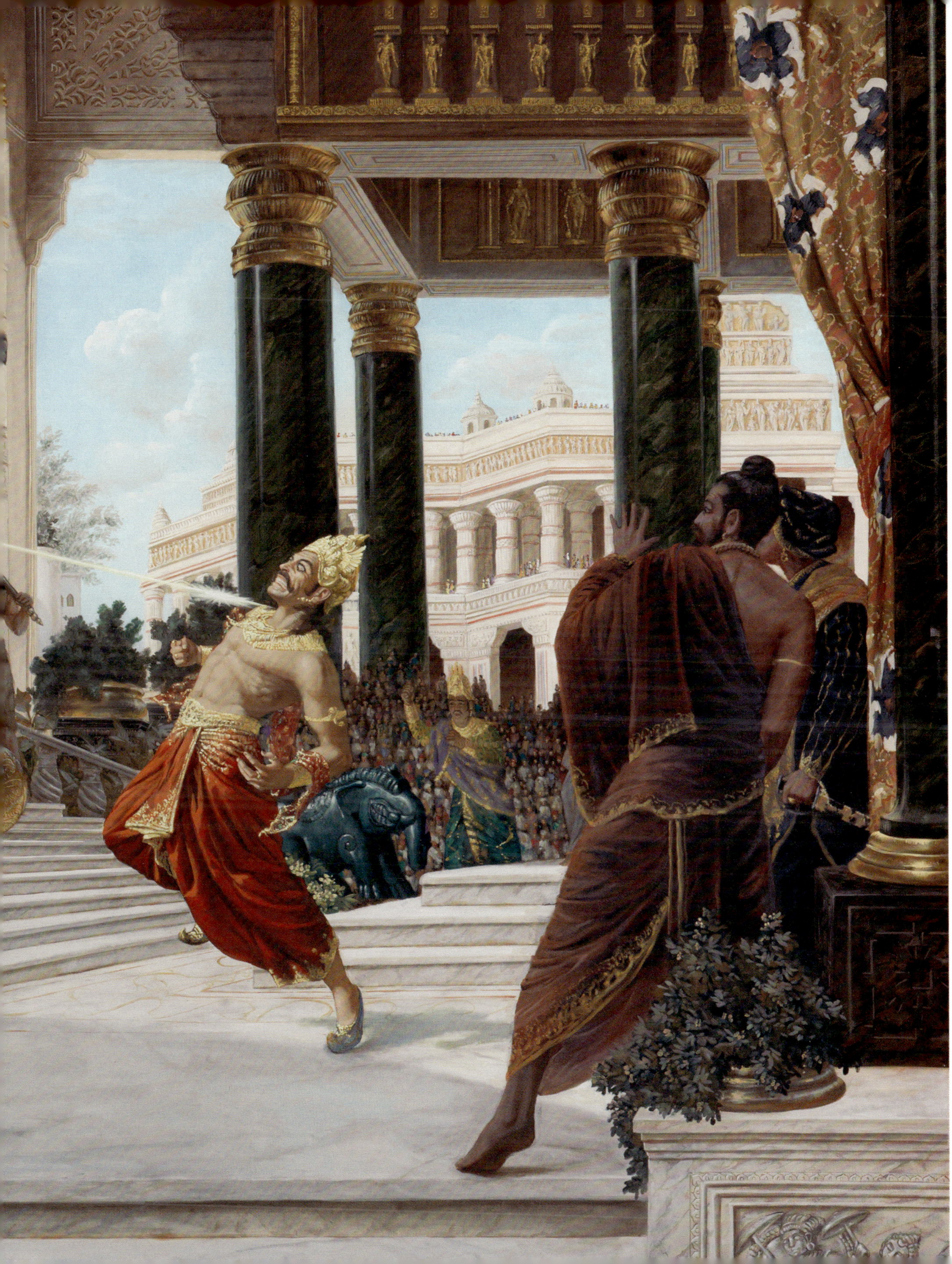

A Strange Charioteer

After the Pandavas accepted Draupadi as their common wife, they had vowed that if any of them entered a room where one of their brothers was alone with her, they would atone by going on pilgrimage for a year. This had happened to Arjuna. He duly set off, and in the course of his travels he reached Dwaraka, the great city in the ocean constructed by Krishna. There he saw Krishna's sister Subhadra, and struck by her matchless beauty, he desired her hand in marriage.

Krishna told his dear friend that it would be difficult for him to promise him Subhadra's hand, because his brother Balarama very much wanted her to marry Duryodhana, Balarama's friend and martial disciple. Arjuna was not to be deterred. He said to Krishna, "Let the girl make her own decision. If she would prefer me, then I will carry her off by force, for this is always the way of heroes." Krishna agreed, and once they had ascertained that Subhadra did indeed want to marry Arjuna rather than Duryodhana or anyone else, a plan was hatched. Krishna would provide him with a chariot, and the Pandava warrior would snatch her away during a festival to be held outside the city. "That will be the best time," Krishna said. "You will be clear of the city guards, and everyone else will be at ease, without weapons."

When the day of the festival arrived, Arjuna got ready. He had been disguised all the while as a sannyasi, and he came unnoticed out of the city. In a secluded spot he changed his dress and put on armour. Krishna met him and gave him a chariot drawn by his celestial steeds. As the Yadus sported and enjoyed themselves in the fragrant woodlands on Raivataka hill outside the city, Arjuna mounted the chariot.

He saw Subhadra surrounded by her friends and maidservants, standing near a temple. Arjuna spurred on the horses and rushed toward the princess. Subhadra looked up in surprise as she heard the clatter of the speeding chariot. She saw Arjuna clutching the reins, a great bow slung on his back and a sword hanging from his belt. The princess smiled in joy. Plainly the Pandava hero was intending to carry her off. She broke free from her companions as he approached, and in less than a minute he had seized her hand and pulled her up onto the chariot. Before anyone could do anything he raced away. As some guards began to give chase, Subhadra took the reins of the chariot so that Arjuna could repel their attack.

The Yadus were infuriated. "Who has dared to kidnap the princess right before our eyes?" they demanded. The word quickly went round that it had

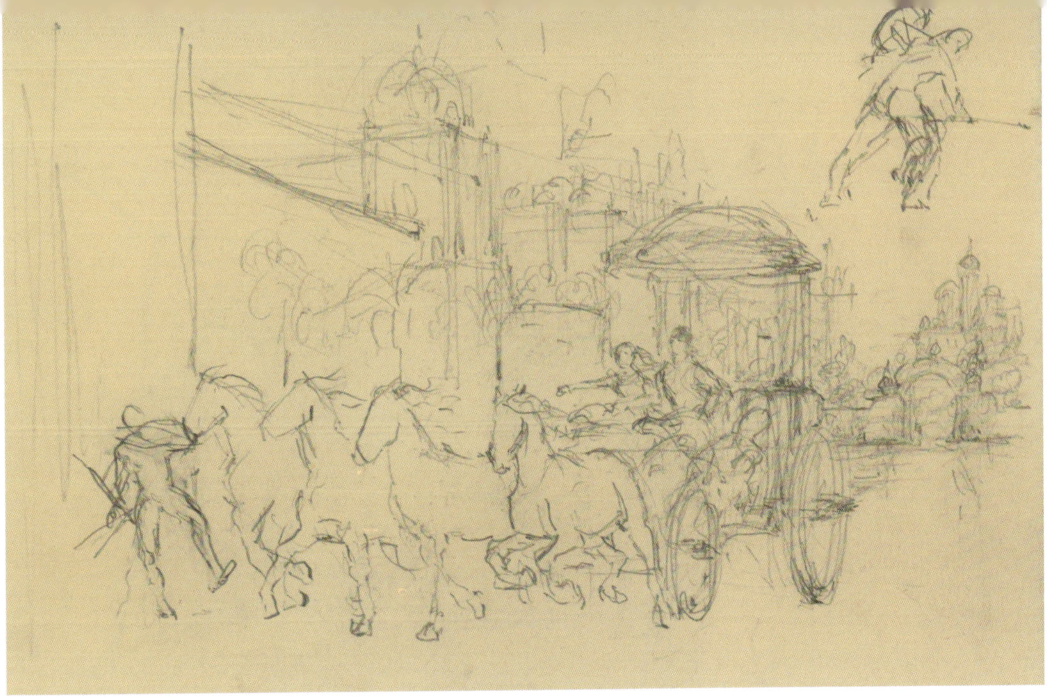

been Arjuna. Hearing this, the Yadu warriors rushed to prepare themselves for a battle. A war council was hastily convened. Many were ready to declare war on Arjuna and his brothers, but Krishna calmed them down. He convinced them that there could be no better husband for Subhadra than Arjuna. Krishna said, "He is the greatest warrior, the son of Kunti, and he is our own kith and kin, sired by the king of the gods. Who would not want him as an ally and a friend?"

Accepting Krishna's words, the Yadus sent messengers after Arjuna. He was brought back and received with honour. The city was decorated with flags and festoons, and a great ceremony took place. Arjuna accepted Subhadra's hand before the sacred fire with the blessings of the sages and city elders. Then he remained in Dwaraka a few more days. Finally, taking permission from Balarama and Krishna, he returned home with his new bride.

A Strange Charioteer
Oil on Canvas, 200 x 250 cm (pp. 60-61)

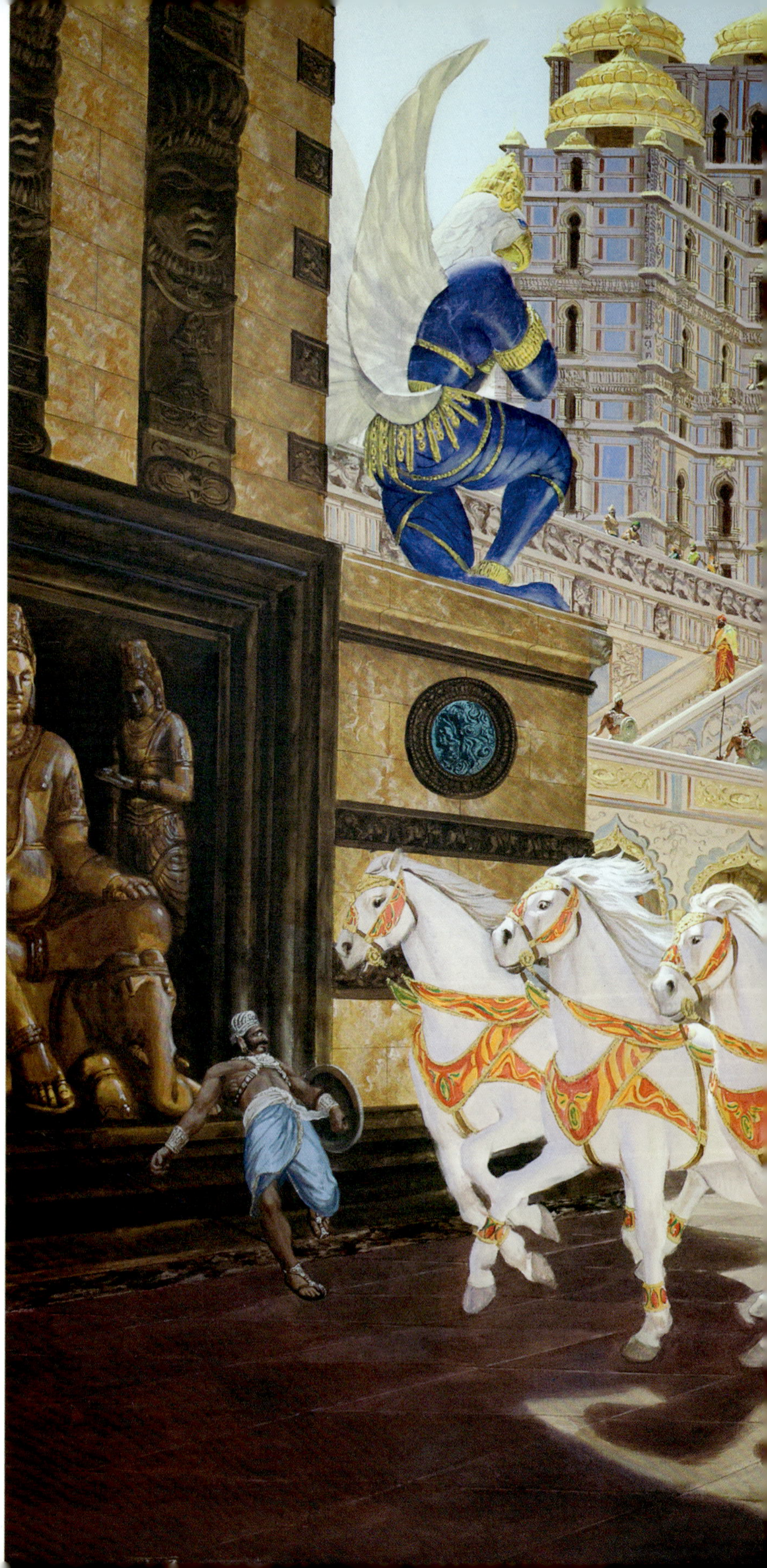

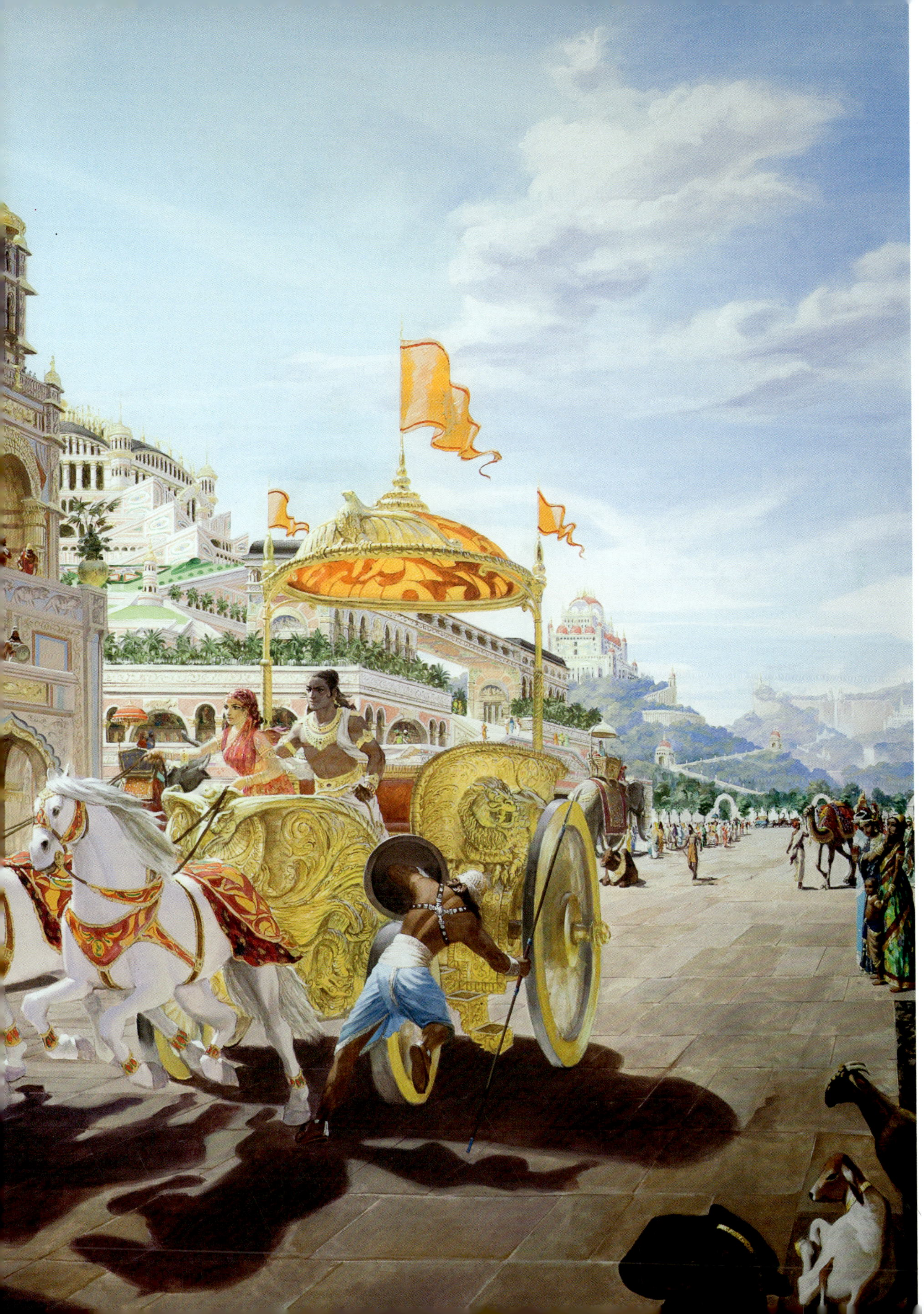

The Pandavas Cheated

To settle the dispute between his sons and the Pandavas, King Dhritarastra divided the Kuru kingdom. He awarded the Pandavas only a barren desert in the northern half, but with Krishna's help they transformed it into the wondrous city of Indraprastha. There they increased their wealth and influence almost unlimitedly, making Duryodhana burn with jealousy. His envy became completely intolerable when he visited an astonishing palace of illusions that had been built for the Pandavas by the celestial artisan, Maya. He fell afoul of the deceptions in the palace to the great amusement of the Pandavas, and he swore vengeance.

In collusion with his brothers and his uncle Shakuni, he arranged a rigged dice match and invited the Pandavas. His plan was to have Shakuni play on his behalf, because his uncle possessed almost mystical powers at dice play and could not be defeated in the game. Yudhisthira's uncle Vidura was sent to invite the Pandavas. Yudishthira understood that some treachery was afoot, but having once vowed to never deny a request from an elder he could not refuse. It was also a duty of heroic warriors to always accept a challenge at gaming or fighting. Seeing all things as a divine arrangement, he said to Vidura, "I shall come, but I fear the outcome. Probably we shall fight, but what can I do? We are all under the Lord's supreme control."

The five brothers arrived in Hastinapura the next day, and soon they were shown into a hall that Duryodhana specially built for the match. When they had taken their seats, Shakuni said, "Welcome, great king. We are eager to play dice with you." Yudhisthira expressed reluctance: "Gambling is fraught with ills, and deceitful gambling is even worse. There is no morality in it, so why do you wish to play?" Shakuni gave a half smile and responded, "We do not desire to play deceitfully. Why do you suggest such a thing? Let us just enjoy a few games with some small stakes. No harm will be done." Yudhisthira replied, "I have no desire to win more wealth, and I do not want to lose the wealth I have, which I use to serve the Brahmins. Why then should I play?" Shakuni looked at Duryodhana and smiled again, saying, "If you are afraid of playing then say so."

The Pandava king saw that his elders were saying nothing, so he said, "I cannot refuse a challenge. This is my vow. Fate is surely all powerful, and whatever is ordained by God will occur without fail." The king asked who would play against him. He said to Shakuni, "I possess limitless wealth, so you are not equal to me." Duryodhana then said that he would provide the stakes, while Shakuni would throw the dice. Yudhisthira's fears were confirmed. This whole situation was engineered to deprive him of his wealth. Still he felt unable to turn back and replied, "Very well, let the game commence."

Yudhisthira removed a priceless pearl necklace and placed that as his stake. Shakuni rolled the dice and soon he was calling out, "Just see, I have won." Again and again the dice were rolled, and again and again Shakuni's voice rang out, "I have won." Gold, gems, land, animals and other kinds of wealth by the millions were staked and lost by Yudhisthira. The game went on for hours, and Shakuni never lost a throw. It seemed as if Yudhisthira were possessed by the desire to lose everything. Finally he had nothing left to stake, but Shakuni goaded him on: "What will you stake now, king?"

To everyone's amazement Yudhisthira said, "Here are my brothers, all obedient to my command. Placing them as my stakes I shall now play." One by one he lost all of his brothers. Duryodhana laughed loudly, enjoying every moment. Shakuni won every game. Finally all that Yudhisthira had to stake was his dear wife, Draupadi. It was still possible for the situation to be reversed, if the Lord desired. He said to the jeering Shakuni, "She who should never be staked I now stake. That most beautiful of women, the divine daughter of Drupada, shall be my final bet. Throw the dice." The hall was filled with kings and princes. All of them stared transfixed at the game as Shakuni rolled the dice. How would this all end? Within moments Shakuni's voice was heard again: "I have won!" As the chaste Draupadi was brought weeping to the assembly, the pious Kuru elders sat shaking their heads with tears streaming from their eyes. The destructive end of their dynasty was now upon them.

The Pandavas Cheated
Oil on Canvas, 70 x 100 cm (pp. 64-65)

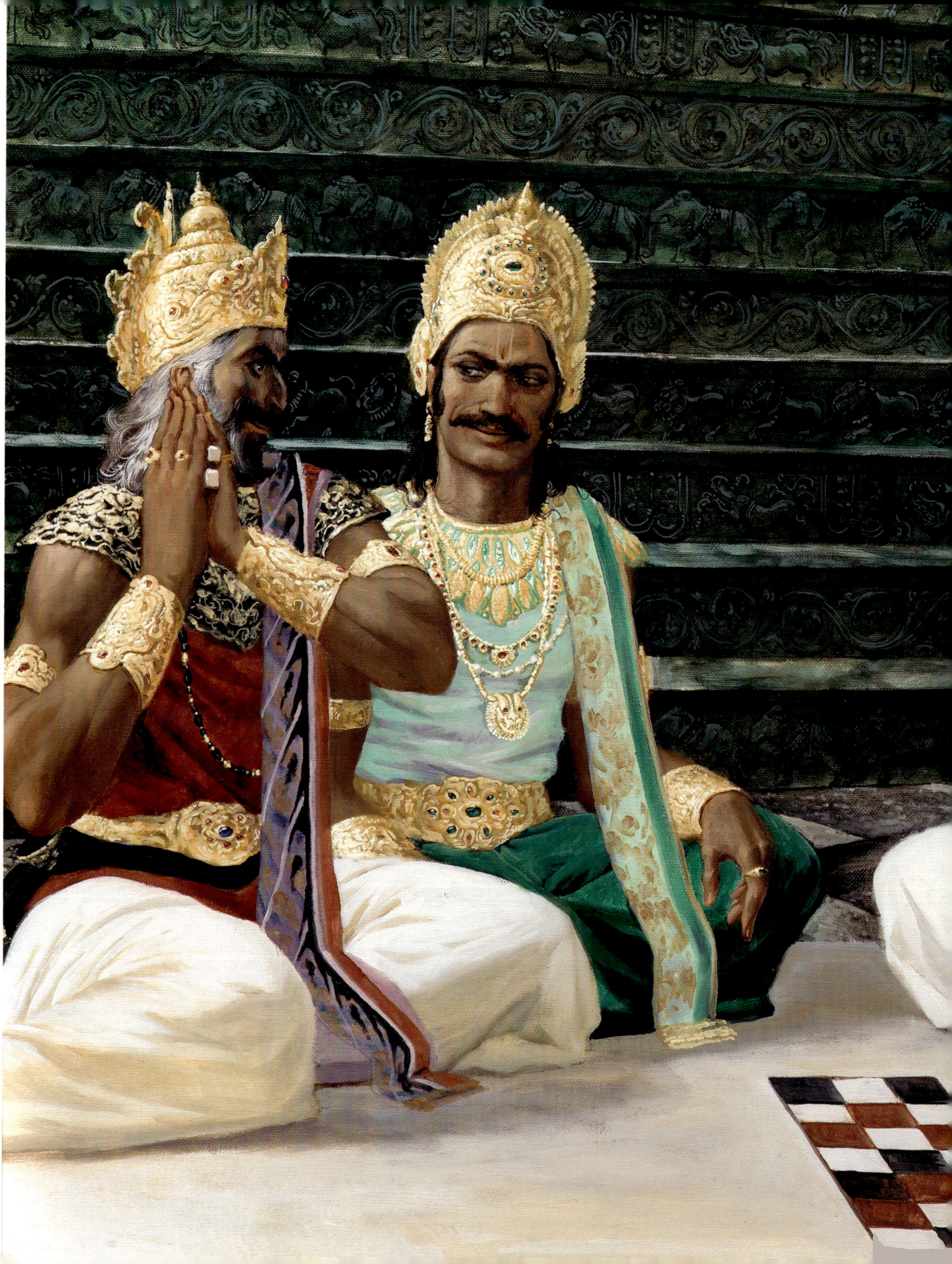

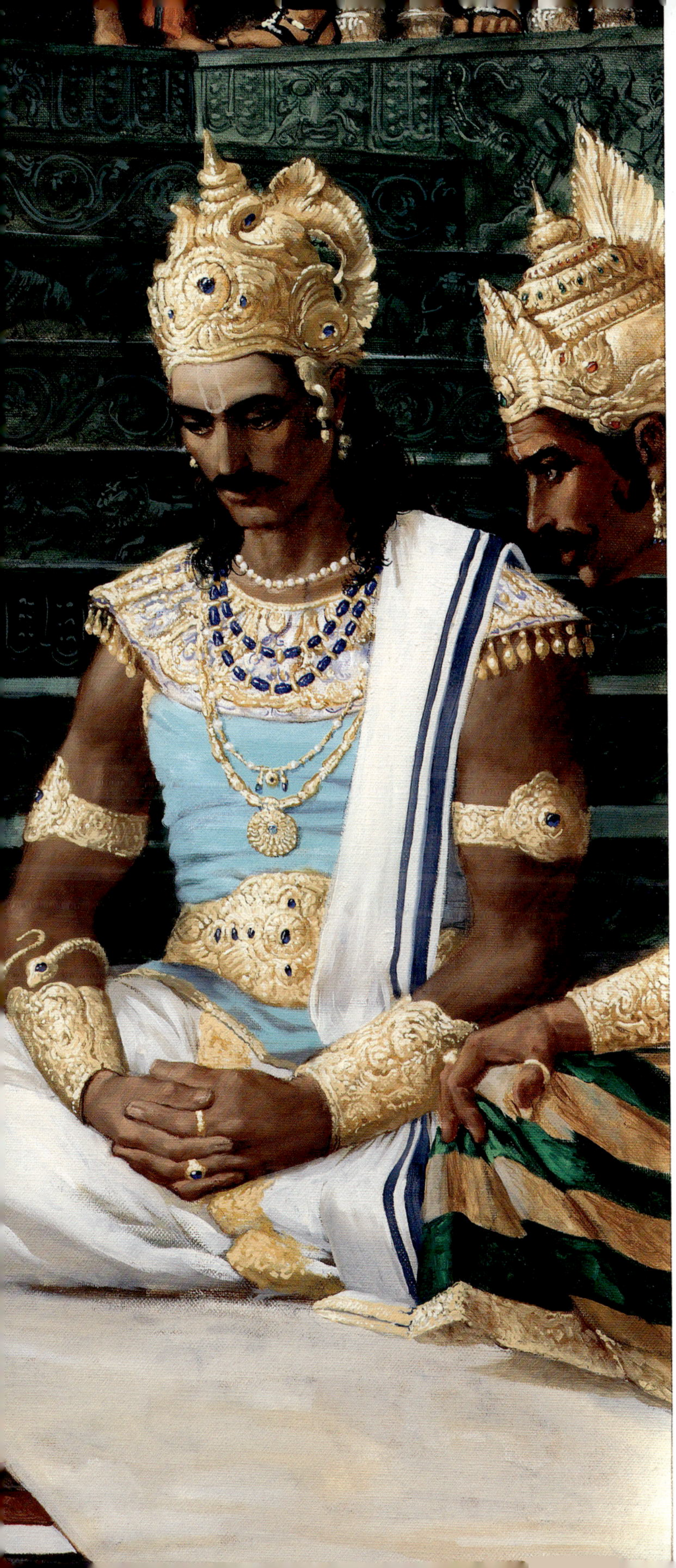

Save My Hounour

When he heard that the Pandavas had been cheated out of their kingdom and wealth in a dishonest game of dice, Krishna, along with his associates, went at once to see them. Accompanied by Balarama and Draupadi's brother, Dhristadyumna, and many other kings, he rode to the Kamayaka forest where they were now dwelling. Seeing them bercft of their royal dress and ornaments and cast out of their home, both Krishna and Balarama were enraged.

Krishna spoke out angrily. "How can this be tolerated? You have been robbed by evil and cunning men. The earth will drink their blood. Duuryodhana, Karna, and all their henchmen will be slain in battle. Then we shall restore Yudhisthira to his rightful position as emperor. This is fully in accord with eternal morality."

Krishna's eyes blazed. It seemed as if he might consume the universe. Quickly Arjuna sought to pacify him by reciting his glories. Arjuna said, "My Lord, you appear on earth for the good of all beings. Hatred and envy do not exist in you. In your many incarnations you establish religion and destroy evil. You have slain many demonic kings who were implacable enemies of the gods." Arjuna described Krishna's transcendental qualities in great ecstasy, naming his divine incarnations and their glorious deeds. Finally, he said, "You are always the well-wisher of all beings. At the end of the millennium all things, mobile and immobile, enter your body. My dear Krishna, your glories have no limit. I have described but a tiny fraction of them. "

Krishna embraced him and said, "You are mine and I am yours. Everything that is mine is also yours. Who hates you, hates me, and who follows you, also follows me." Krishna said that Arjuna had formerly been the sage Nara and that he himself was Narayana: "Although individuals in two bodies, we are one. None can understand our oneness and difference."

Seeing Krishna in a milder mood, Draupadi expressed concern. She wanted her honour to be avenged. Coming forward with folded palms, she said, "Dear Krishna, great sages say you are the Supreme Person, within whom the entire

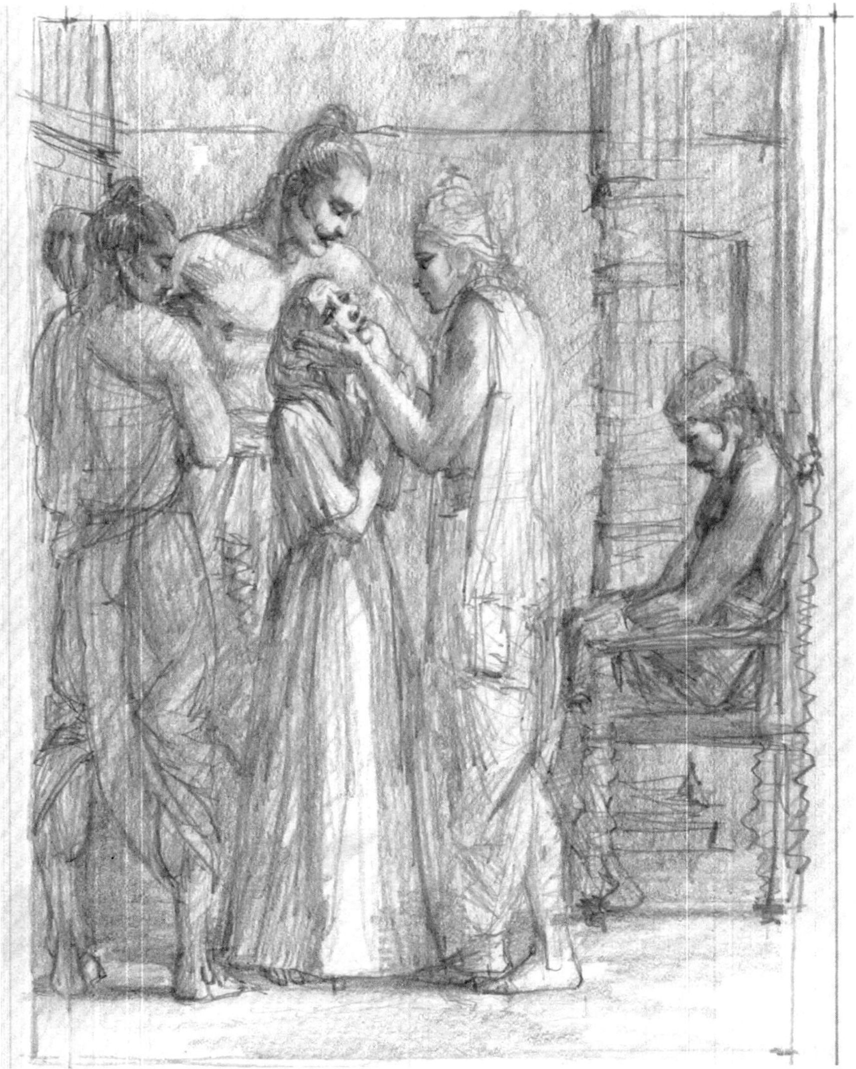

universe exists. Those seeking your protection are never destroyed. How then were the wicked Kauravas able to insult me, the wife of the Pandavas, and your friend and devotee?" Draupadi wept as she spoke, describing her grief and anger. She looked at Krishna and said, "I deserve your protection for four reasons; as your relative, as your friend, as your devotee and out of the respect your bear for me."

Krishna placed a reassuring hand on Draupadi's shoulder and said, "Dear lady, the wives of those who have made you weep will also weep even as you do now. They will see their husbands lying dead on the battlefield, covered in arrows and soaked in blood." Krishna assured her that the Pandavas would regain their kingdom and she would be their queen. "I speak the truth. The heavens may fall, the Himalayas may move, the earth may be rent, and the ocean may dry up, but my words shall not fail."

Draupadi felt solaced. She knew that Krishna acted only for her good. Arjuna also reassured her, "Do not weep, princess. What Krishna has said will surely come to pass." The other kings voiced their agreement, saying that they would all fight in the forthcoming battle. Having pledged their commitment to the Pandavas, they left for their own kingdoms.

Save My Honour
Oil on Canvas, 160 x 120 cm

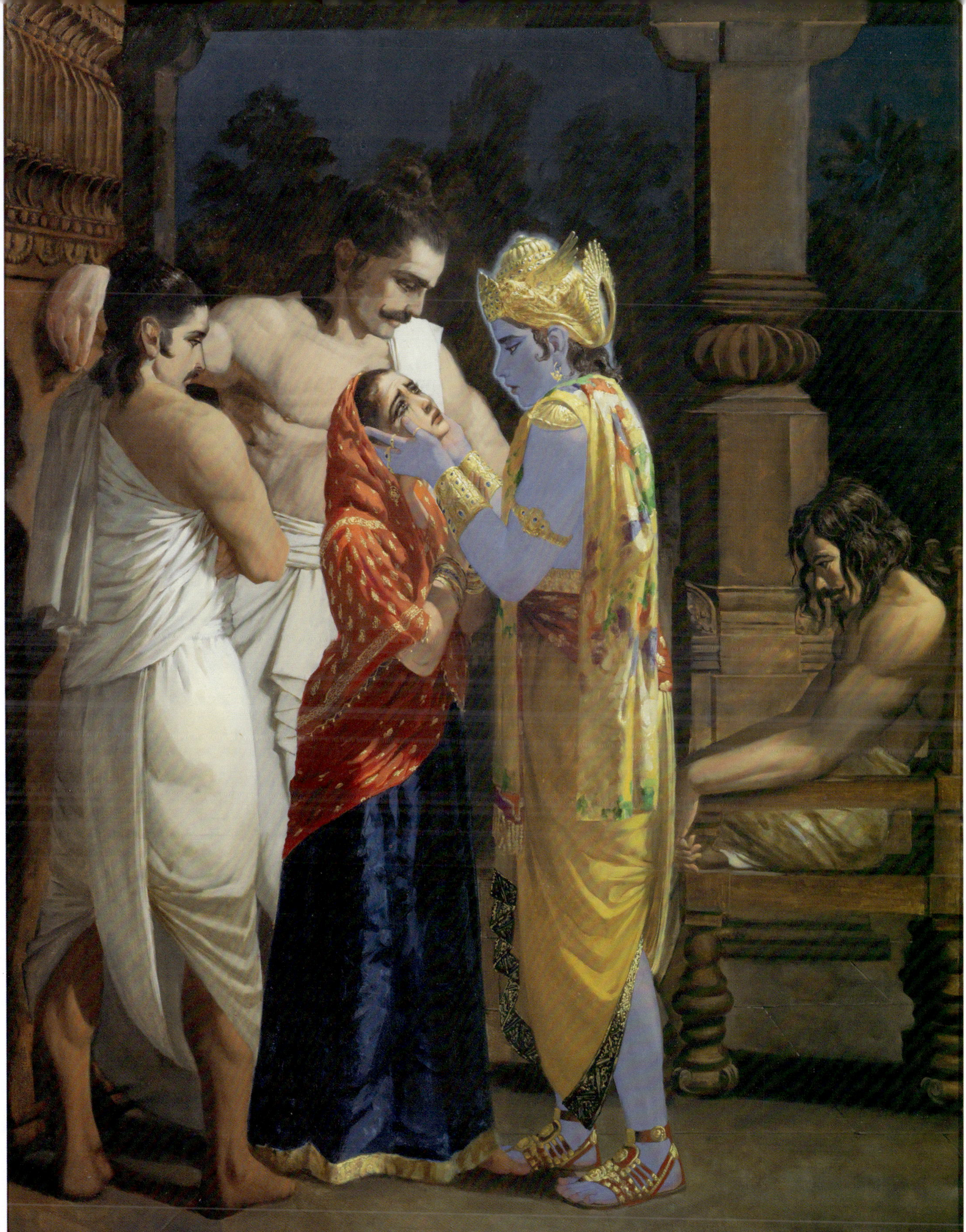

O Brother! Bhima and Hanuman

Almost ten years of the Pandavas' exile in the forest had passed. Arjuna was away in the heavens to procure weapons for the inevitable war with the Kauravas, and Draupadi was especially missing him. One day, while she was sitting in their humble forest cottage, an unusual flower fell at her feet. It was a golden lotus with a thousand petals, which had been carried by the wind from a celestial region high in the mountains. Charmed by its beauty and delightful fragrance, Draupadi showed it to Bhima. "Just see this wonderful flower," she said. "O Bhima, if only I had more of these that I could offer them to Yudhisthira. Surely they would cheer him up."

Draupadi looked longingly at Bhima, who felt enlivened to comply with her request. He was glad for the opportunity to please his beloved wife, who had suffered greatly since they had gone to the forest. Without delay he turned he set off at a fast pace and bounded up the hill. As he leapt from crag to crag, pulling himself up with his mighty arms, Bhima shouted in exultation. His powerful voice boomed around the mountain, scaring the animals, who fled. As he reached the higher plateaus he saw the celestial Siddhas and Charanas sporting with their consorts in flower-filled meadows. He saw many charming lakes, but did not see the golden lotuses.

Continuing upwards, he suddenly heard a tremendous sound from somewhere ahead. It seemed as if an immense, powerful being was pounding the earth and causing it to tremble. Trees shook, and their fruits fell to the ground. Fearlessly Bhima plunged on, and as he burst into a clearing he came upon a huge monkey lying beside the path. This creature resembled a hill, with broad shoulders, narrow waist and his long tail stretched across the path. He was lashing his tail, which was producing the terrific sound Bhima had heard. He appeared to be sleeping, but as Bhima approached, he opened his eyes and said, "You cannot proceed further. This path leads to heaven. Only those with pious merits can go there. Therefore rest awhile if it pleases you, and then return the way you came."

Bhima respectfully asked, "Who are you, sir, lying here in the form of a monkey? Know me to be Bhima, son of Kunti and Pandu, begotten by Vayu." The monkey looked at him languidly and said, "I am just a monkey, but I cannot let you pass. Please turn back or you will needlessly meet with destruction." Bhima laughed. "I am not seeking your permission. This mountain belongs to no one, and I intend to continue. Please give me way." The monkey

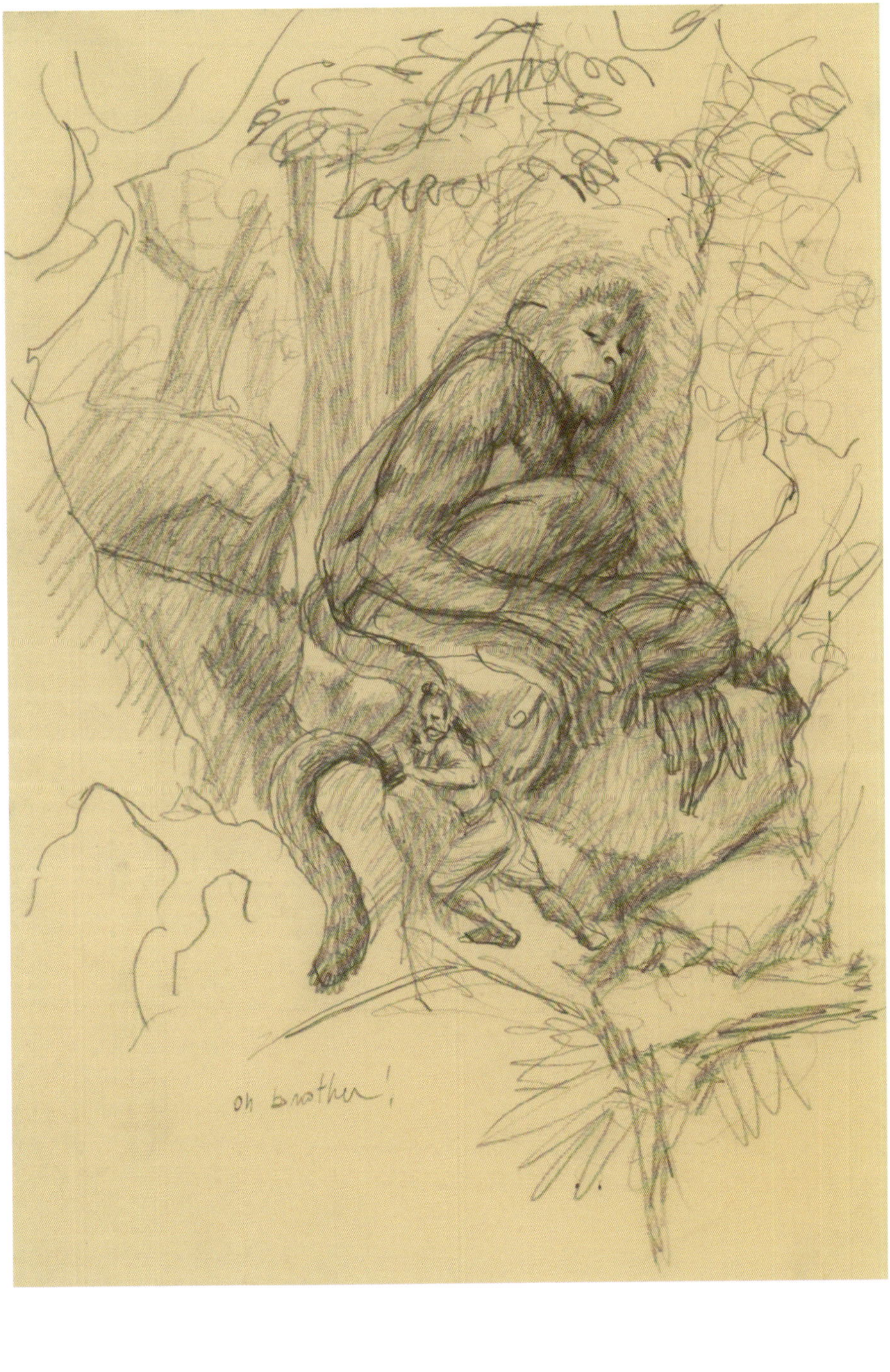
oh brother!

said, "Very well, if you must get past me, then step over my tail. I am too tired to move it." Bhima could not do that. He said, "I will not offend the Lord in any creature's heart by stepping over him."

So he bent down and seized hold of the monkey's tail casually with one hand, intending to move it aside. To his amazement he could not move it even slightly. Tightening his cloth, he reached down with both hands and began to exert his full power. He struggled and strained and tried his very best to move the tail, but without success. It was immovable.

Bhima looked up in awe and asked, "Who are you? I do not think you can be an ordinary monkey or even a demon. Are you a god?" Laughing, the monkey said, "Know me to be Hanuman, son of Vayu and Keshari. Bhima fell flat before him in obeisance. He said, "How greatly fortunate I am to meet you, my most powerful and famous brother."

The two brothers spoke for some time, and Hanuman showed him the tremendous form with which he had leapt over the ocean many years before. He then offered to assist Bhima in the fight against the Kauravas. "Just ask and I will slay them all and grind their city to dust." Bhima thanked him, but said that his mere blessings would be enough to ensure their victory. Hanuman promised to appear on Arjuna's flag to support the Pandavas when the war finally came. After this he showed Bhima the way to the lotus lake he was seeking and then vanished.

O Brother! Bhima and Hanuman
Oil on Canvas, 170 x 120 cm

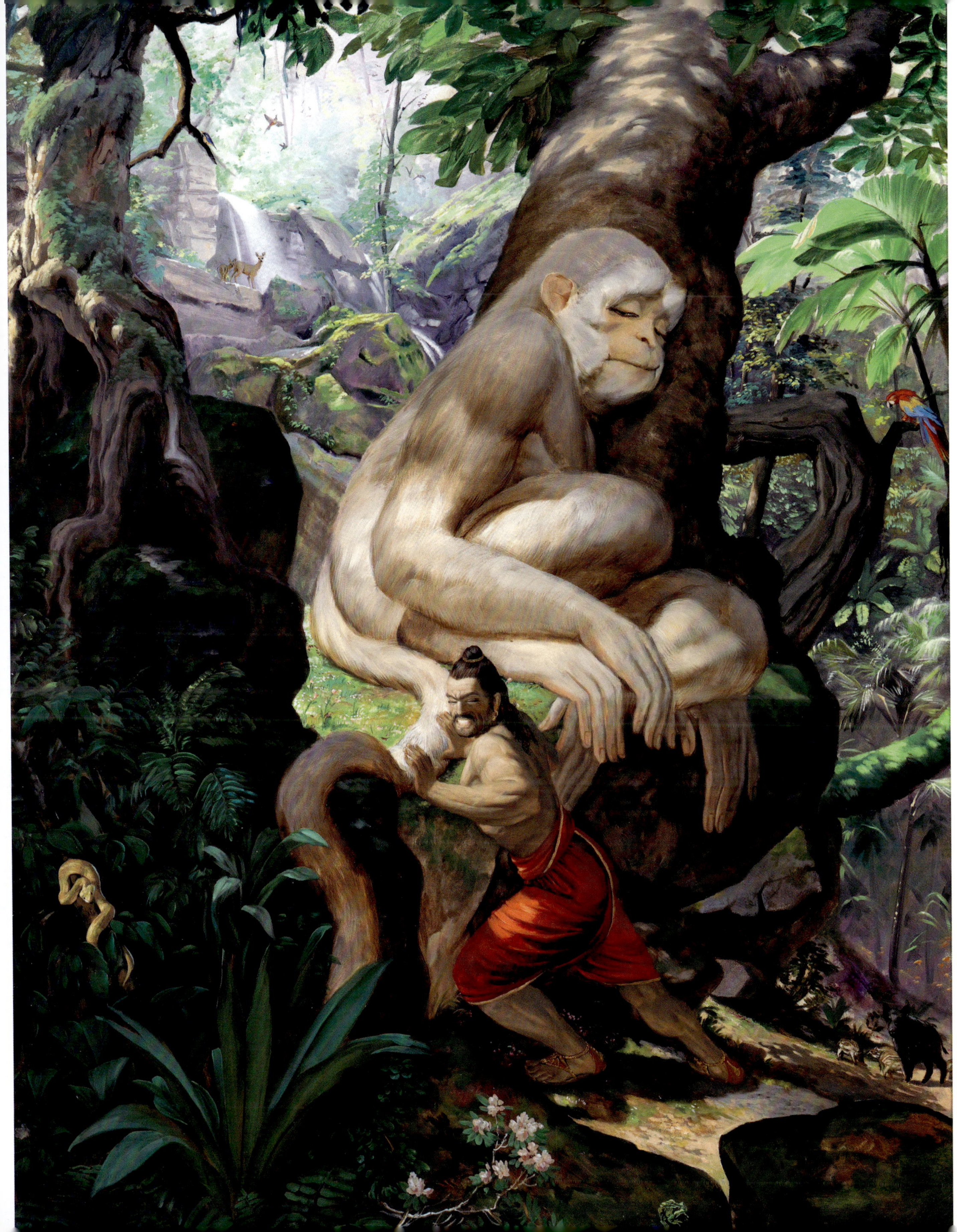

The Universal Form (Vishvarupa)

The Pandavas had finally emerged from their exile. Thirteen years had passed, as agreed at the fateful dice match where they lost everything: twelve years in the forest and the final year incognito in Virat, where they now waited for Duryodhana's next move. No word had come from the Kaurava prince, and the Pandavas knew that war was imminent. News had reached them that the Kauravas were amassing a vast army.

The final reckoning was fast approaching, but Yudhisthira wanted to give peace one last chance. The humble Pandava monarch was prepared to accept just five villages. Perhaps Duryodhana would agree to that proposal. A messenger was sent, but the reply came back that the Pandavas would be given nothing. Among Yudhisthira's friends and allies who came to Virat to offer him their support was Krishna. After hearing the Kaurava's reply he said, "On Yudhisthira's behalf I shall go to the Kauravas and try to persuade them that it is the duty of sane men to avert war if it lies in their power, and I shall do all I can to save the world's warriors from a needless slaughter."

Yudhisthira was hesitant to let Krishna go, knowing that Duryodhana could not be trusted in any way. Out of love for Krishna he said, "Surely he will try to harm you." Krishna laughed and said, "There exists no power in this world that can harm me, dear friend. If Duryodhana tries anything, I will show him my prowess and end his life on this earth along with the lives of his allies."

After reassuring Yudhisthira, Krishna set off for Hastinapura on his peace mission. Coming before the Kauravas in their assembly hall, he began to make his case: "Let there be peace among all you brothers. Why fight? The Pandavas will happily share with you whatever they have. There need not be any dispute."

Duryodhana hated the Pandavas. He envied their power and their popularity. There was no possibility he would give them anything, and he made this clear to Krishna: "You should know that I will not relinquish to the Pandavas even as much land as one can drive a needle into." The angry prince then stormed out of the hall.

He went at once to his friends with whom he had hatched a plan. The Kaurava princes knew that, without Krishna, the Pandavas would be stricken and easily defeated. They had therefore concluded that their best hope was to kidnap Krishna and prevent his return to the Pandavas. This plot had become known to their father, the blind King Dhritarastra. Although he also wanted to keep the kingdom from the Pandavas, he was horrified by his sons' intentions. So he ordered, "Bring Duryodhana back at once," and the smirking prince duly returned.

Dhritarastra privately condemned him for his insane plan to capture Krishna, but the prince said nothing. Other Kuru elders tried to dissuade him, but even as they spoke Krishna rose up and said, "Listen to me Duryodhana. In your madness you think me weak and vulnerable. See now the truth. Here are all the gods, the Adityas, Rudras, Vasus and the great sages. See too the mighty heroes of my armies and my family."

Duryodhana snorted. Leaping up from his seat he shouted, "Seize him at once!" Soldiers ran into the hall wielding weapons and tried to approach Krishna, who merely laughed. His body flashed like lightning and grew to a tremendous size. From his forehead appeared the four headed Brahma and from his chest came Shiva. On his huge arms were the Lokapalas, the guardians of the four directions of the universe. The fire-god sprang from his mouth, and from his waist appeared Indra, along with great hosts of Gandharvas, Yakshas, and Rakshasas. The five Pandavas stood around him, as well as Balarama and his many sons and other relatives, headed by the invincible Pradyumna. His personal weapons (the mace, discus, and club) also appeared there, blazing with terrible brilliance. Krishna's body emanated light, sparks, and great clouds of smoke.

Everyone but a few of Krishna's devotees closed their eyes in terror. From the heavens, drums sounded and flowers fell. As the great sages offered Krishna their prayers, he gradually withdrew his mystical form. Without a word, he stood up and left the hall before the amazed eyes of Duryodhana and his brothers. Their plan to kidnap him was plainly futile.

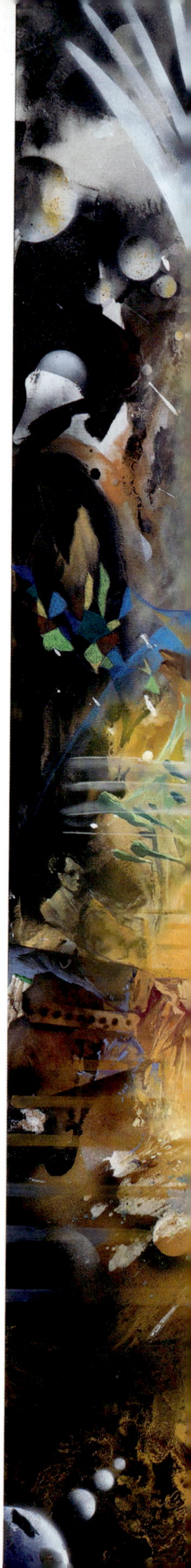

The Universal Form (Vishvarupa)
Oil on Canvas, 200 x 200 cm

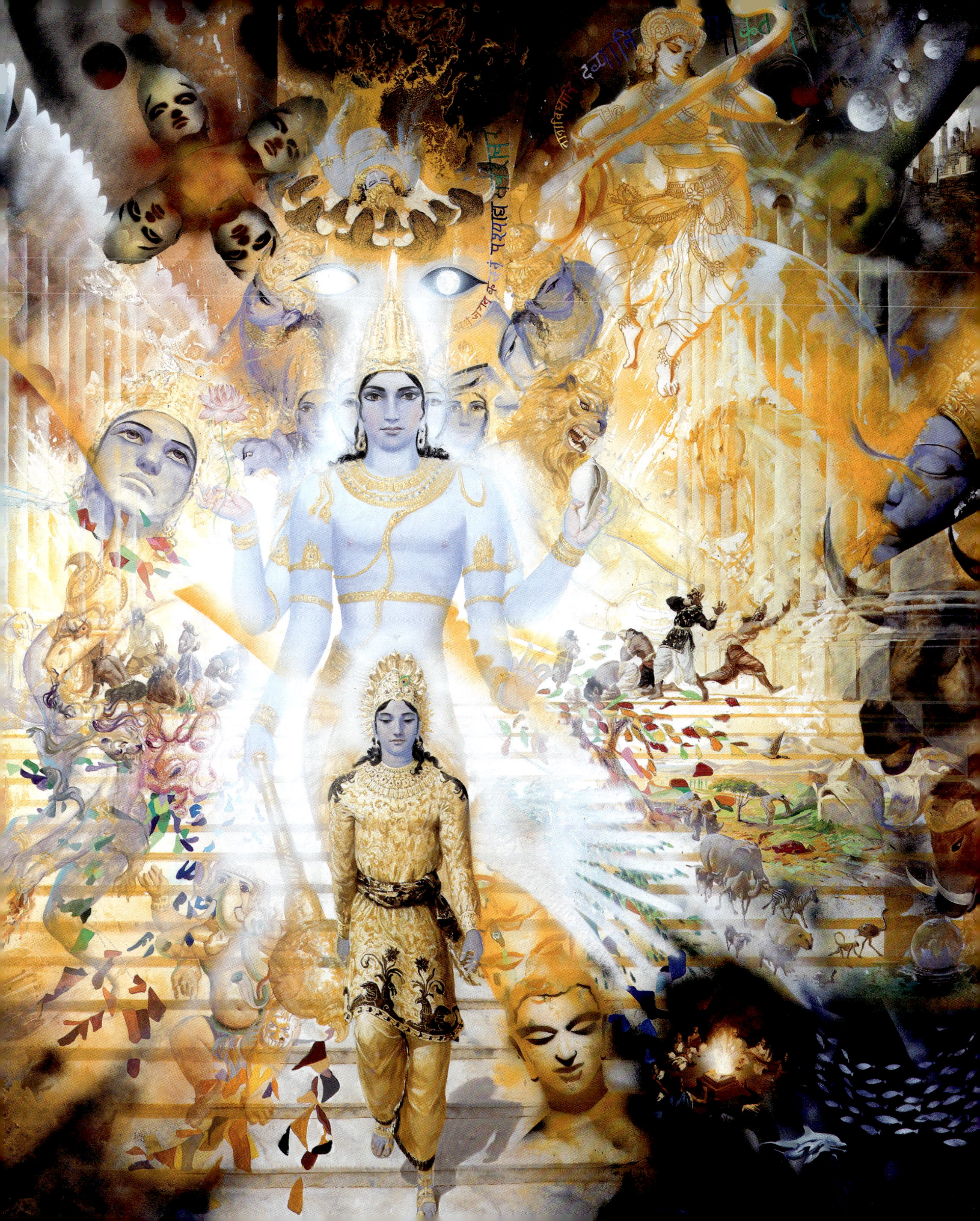

Karna and Kunti

The time had finally come for the long awaited war between the Pandavas and Kauravas. All attempts at negotiations had failed and the two sides began to prepare for battle. When she heard this Kunti was stricken with fear. Her first son Karna had sided with the Kauravas against her other five sons. Although she had been forced to abandon him at birth, she had never stopped loving him. She knew that now either he or her other sons would be killed. Perhaps though if he understood his true lineage, how he was a brother to the Pandavas, he would switch sides. Kunti decided to tell him.

Karna had always felt an attraction for the sun-god, even without knowing he was his father. Each day he would go to the banks of the Ganga and offer worship to the deity. On the morning that Kunti decided to reveal that she was his mother he went as usual to the river and stood waist deep in the water worshipping Surya with folded palms. Kunti watched him from the bank as he chanted his mantras to the rising sun. Finally he turned to return to the bank and saw Kunti.

Karna bowed in respect and said, "You are most welcome, noble lady. Know me to be Karna, son of Adhiratha and Radha. What brings you here?" Kunti looked at her son with tears welling up in her eyes. It was difficult for her to speak. Gradually she composed herself and began to speak softly. "Dear child, please know that you are not the son of Adhiratha. I am your mother. You were conceived by the great sun-god Surya upon myself. Born with celestial armour and earrings, you shone like your celestial father."Kunti looked down, feeling ashamed as she went on, "Although it broke my heart I could not keep you. Out of fear for mine and my father's reputation I cast you adrift upon this river. You were then found and adopted by Adhiratha." Karna looked at her in disbelief. Why had she never told him before? Was this just a ploy to make him abandon Duryodhana in order to assist the Pandavas? That seemed unlikely.

Kunti was famous for her virtue. She could not be lying. As the truth sank in Karna's mind was in turmoil. He gazed at Kunti unable to make any reply. Kunti continued, "Know that you are the elder brother of the Pandavas. Do not be misled by wicked men like Duryodhana. Join with your brothers and end the war now. Who would oppose you when you stand with Arjuna? Dear child, you are a great hero of the warrior class. Do not again call yourself a son of a charioteer." As Kunti finished speaking a voice was heard coming

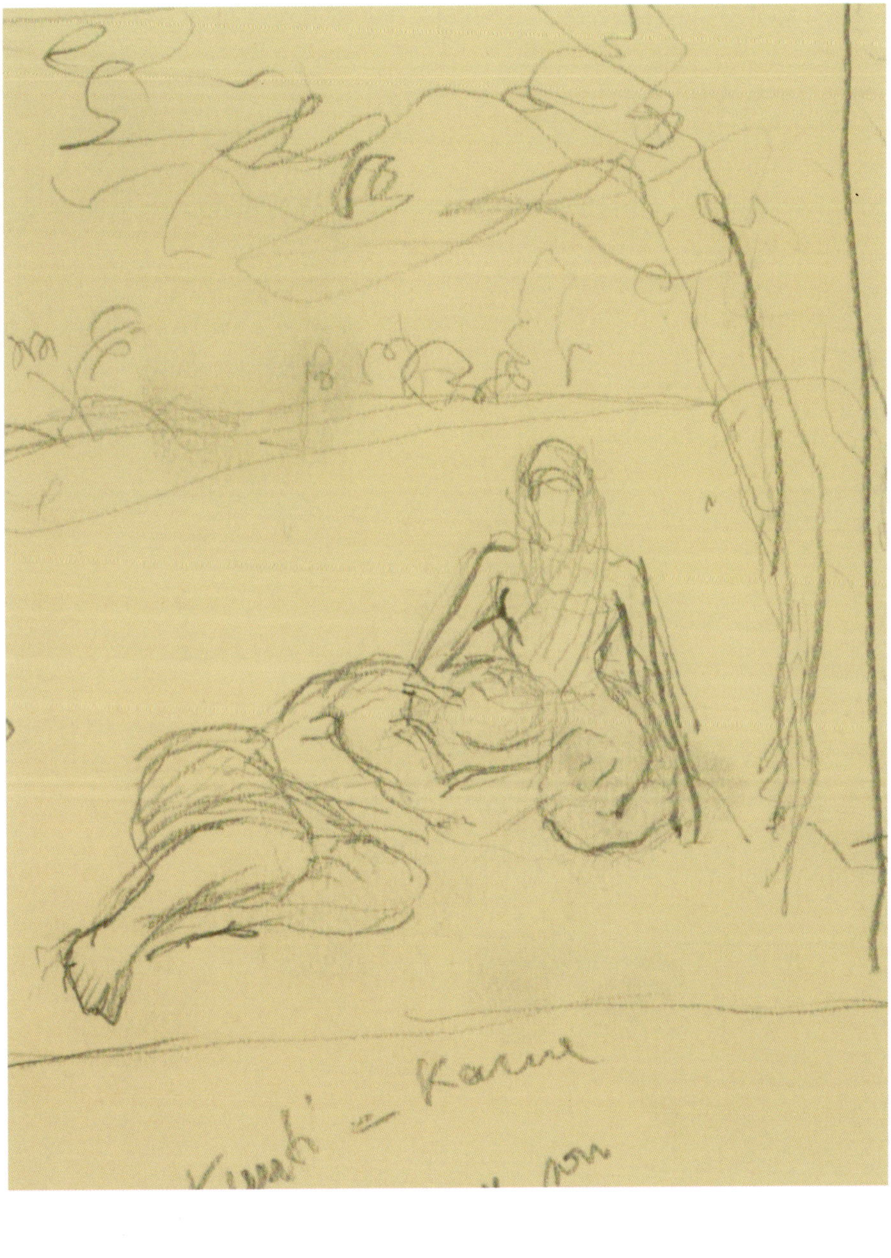

from the sun, "Kunti speaks the truth. Take her advice, Karna, for it will be in your best interests." Karna took a deep breath and gathered his wits about him. He said, "I do not doubt your words, gentle lady. Adhiratha himself told me he had found me adrift on the river. How though can I accept that you are my well-wisher after you abandoned me at birth? How too can I now abandon Duryodhana who, unlike yourself and your other sons, has shown me so much love?"

Karna was torn, especially after hearing the words from the sun-god, but he made a firm decision. "I shall not swerve now from my obligation to the Kauravas. But I say this; in the great war to come I shall only kill one of my brothers, and that will be Arjuna. You shall still have five sons, for either he or I will not return from the fight alive." After uttering these words, Karna stepped forward to embrace his mother, Kunti, with tears streaming down his face. But it was too late now for both of them. There was no turning back.

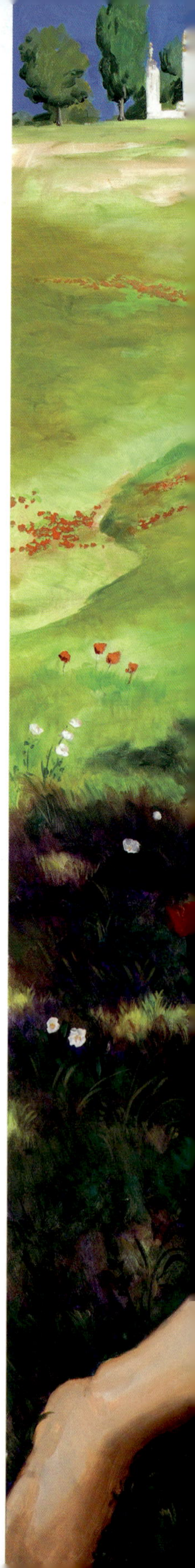

Karna and Kunti
Oil on canvas, 150 x 150 cm

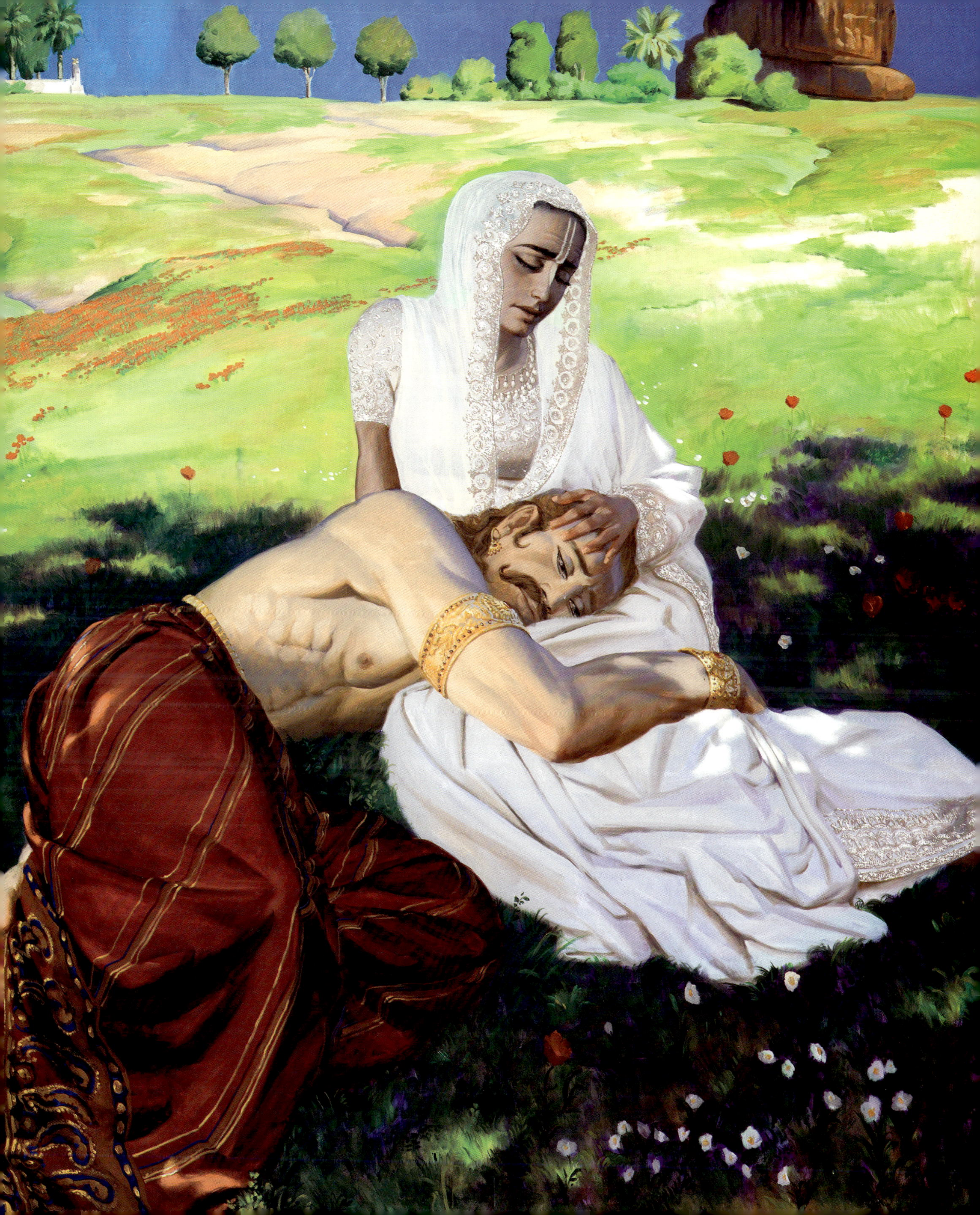

The Choice

Having emerged from exile the Pandavas realised that war was now inevitable. They heard that Duryodhana was already assembling a vast army. He had despatched messengers to all parts of the world seeking the support of other kings. The Pandavas also sent out their own emissaries to their various allies, asking them to prepare for war. Krishna had come to Virat to see the Pandavas, but had gone back to Dwaraka to await further developments. At that time both Arjuna and Duryodhana decided to ask for his assistance in the war. They both set off in swift chariots for Dwaraka.

The first to arrive was Duryodhana. Reaching Krishna's palace he leapt down from his steed and was respectfully greeted by the guards who led him into the bejewelled, marble mansion. Arjuna arrived minutes later and was similarly shown in by the guards. As he reached Krishna's bedchamber he saw Duryodhana standing their with a smile on his face. He guessed that Arjuna had come with the same intention as him, but the proper etiquette was that a warrior would accept the first person who approached him for support, and that was Duryodhana. He greeted Arjuna amiably and the two men entered the room. They saw Krishna resting on a great silken bed, being fanned by Rukmini. Duryodhana went up to the head of the bed and sat on a fine chair to wait for him to awake.

Arjuna waited at the foot of the bed admiring his beloved Lord. Krishna seemed like a slumbering lion as he lay peacefully upon the golden bed. His beautiful features completely captivated Arjuna's heart and he simply stood gazing at him. Gradually the Lord stirred and opened his eyes. Seeing both Arjuna and Duryodhana he sat up and greeted them both and asked what had brought them. Duryodhana said, "My dear Krishna, we have both come seeking your assistance in the war that will soon ensue. You are Arjuna's friend, but as you should know that I arrived here first." Krishna smiled and said, "I accept that you were first to arrive, but I saw Arjuna first so I must assist both of you. Furthermore, he is younger than you so it is proper that I should allow him take first choice. I have an army of one million soldiers equal in power to myself which one of you may have. Then there is myself, who will go alone to the other side, but I shall not fight. My weapons will be laid aside for the entire battle." Duryodhana looked alarmed. He was about to voice his objections but Arjuna immediately said, "I choose you, Krishna." Duryodhana sighed inwardly. Arjuna's affection for his friend had plainly

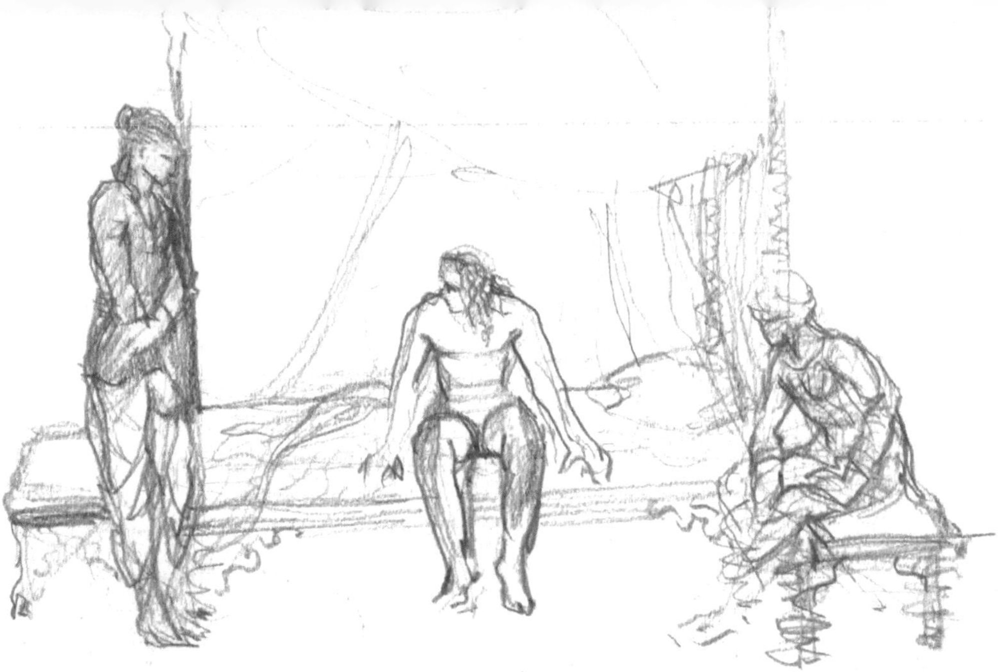

clouded his better judgment. Smiling slightly Duryodhana said, "It seems I am left with the army rather than yourself. That is my misfortune. Pray grant me your permission dear Krishna and I shall depart."

After Duryodhana had left Krishna said to Arjuna, "Why did you choose me over the army?" Arjuna said, "With you on my side victory is certain whether or not you fight. Your mere presence is the assurance of all success. Doubtlessly by your grace I shall gain great fame in this war, but what I most want is your association." Arjuna's eyes welled with tears as he went on, "I have long desired that you act as my charioteer. If it is also your desire, dear friend, please take that position in the coming war." Placing a hand on Arjuna's shoulder Krishna said, "I shall gladly accept that role. Let your desire be fulfilled."

The Choice
Oil on Canvas, 180 x 230 cm (pp. 84-85)

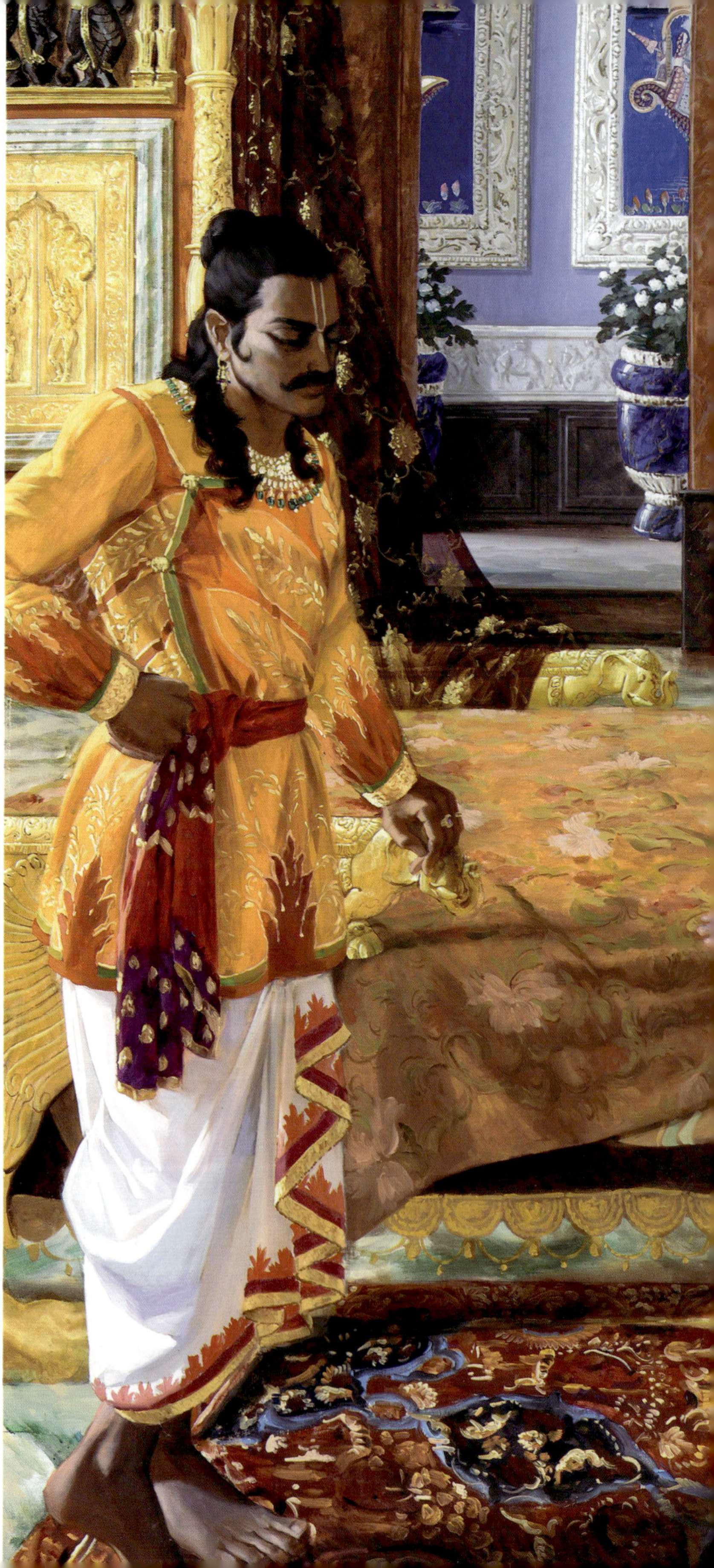

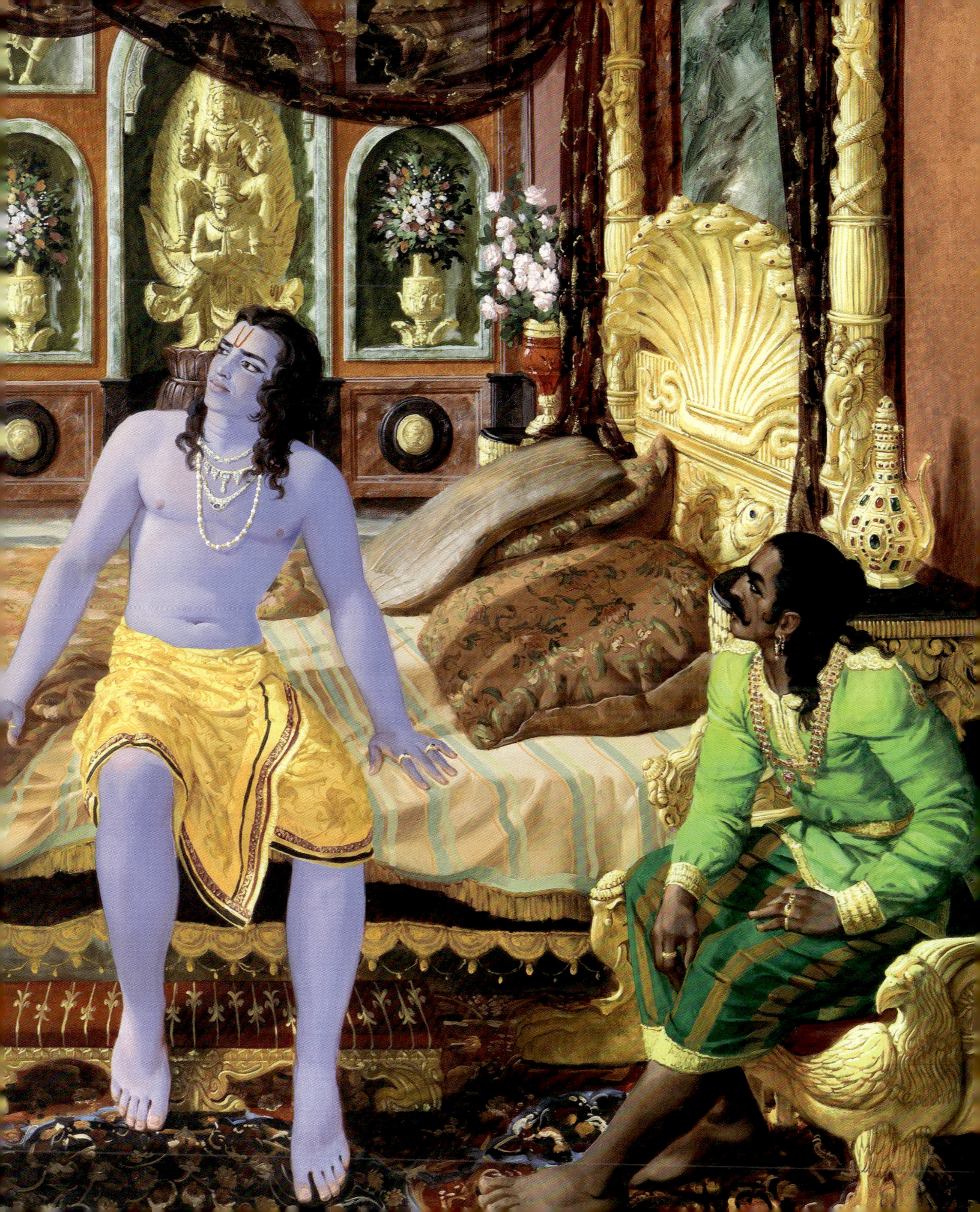

Parthasarathi

The first manoeuvres of the battle had commenced. Both armies began to position themselves ready for the order to fight. Krishna had taken the reins of Arjuna's chariot and he stationed it at the front of the army. Gazing out at the vast array of men, chariots, horses and elephants, Arjuna said, "My dear Krishna, please go closer to the Kauravas. I wish to see who has come to fight with us today, wanting to please the evil-minded Duryodhana."

Krishna immediately complied and the great chariot rolled forward with a thunderous rumble. Coming between the two armies he smilingly said, "See here the Kurus who are assembled for battle, Arjuna." Arjuna looked across at the opposing army with all its familiar faces. There he could see the invincible Bhishma, who had always been like an affectionate father to him. He saw his beloved guru Drona and his old teacher Kripa. Lined up with weapons at the ready were all kinds of friends and relatives arrayed for battle. As the enormity of the situation sank in Arjuna began to tremble.

He now faced the prospect of seeing them all slain, many of them no doubt by him. It was hardly conscionable. Shedding tears of compassion he said, "Krishna, seeing all these men here in such a fighting spirit I am hardly able to move. My limbs are afflicted with weakness and my mouth is drying up." Krishna listened in silence as his friend continued. "What good could possibly ensue from killing my relations, dear Krishna? Will it not be sinful? I don't even want the kingdom, especially at the cost of great personalities like Bhishma and Drona. It surely can't be virtuous to gain wealth by killing such men." Arjuna's bow slipped from his hand and he dropped to his knees. There was no question of continuing. He declared himself unable to fight. It would be better if the Kauravas killed him unarmed and unresisting than face the prospect of slaying so many loved ones. Arjuna looked up at Krishna and said, "I do not think it proper to fight, yet I know it is my duty. My mind is completely perplexed."

Still smiling, Krishna said, "My dear Arjuna, this is simply weakness of heart on your part. You are being overwhelmed by false conceptions." Arjuna could not understand what Krishna meant, but he knew him to be the greatest authority. He said, "My Lord, I surrender to you as your disciple. Please instruct me. I shall do whatever you say." Krishna then delivered the Bhagavad-gita to Arjuna, instructing him about the nature of the soul, time, karma, the material energy and God.

He explained that all of Arjuna's arguments against fighting were based upon the false ego of bodily identification and sense gratification. He had failed to recognise the higher principle of ultimate spiritual welfare, which depended upon following God's will and desire. Any action or indeed inaction not based upon this principle was inauspicious and would lead only to suffering. Making it clear that he wanted Arjuna to fight, Krishna said, "With your mind fixed on me, go into battle for my pleasure. Abandon all attachment to the result, whether it be good or bad in your estimation. In this way you will attain the highest goal of life, my eternal spiritual abode." Krishna told Arjuna to give up all other ideas of religion other than what he, the Supreme Lord, personally desired.

There was nothing superior to this, for ultimately religion came from him and all its results were awarded by him. Arjuna understood that he had been deluded. Krishna was right. His whole approach had been based on the bodily conception of life. He said, "Dear Krishna, my illusion is now dispelled. You are the Supreme Truth and I totally accept everything you say. I will now fight in full accordance with your direction." Taking up his bow again, Arjuna prepared for battle as Krishna brought his chariot back to the front of the army.

Parthasarathi
Oil on Canvas, 200 x 300 cm (pp. 88-89)

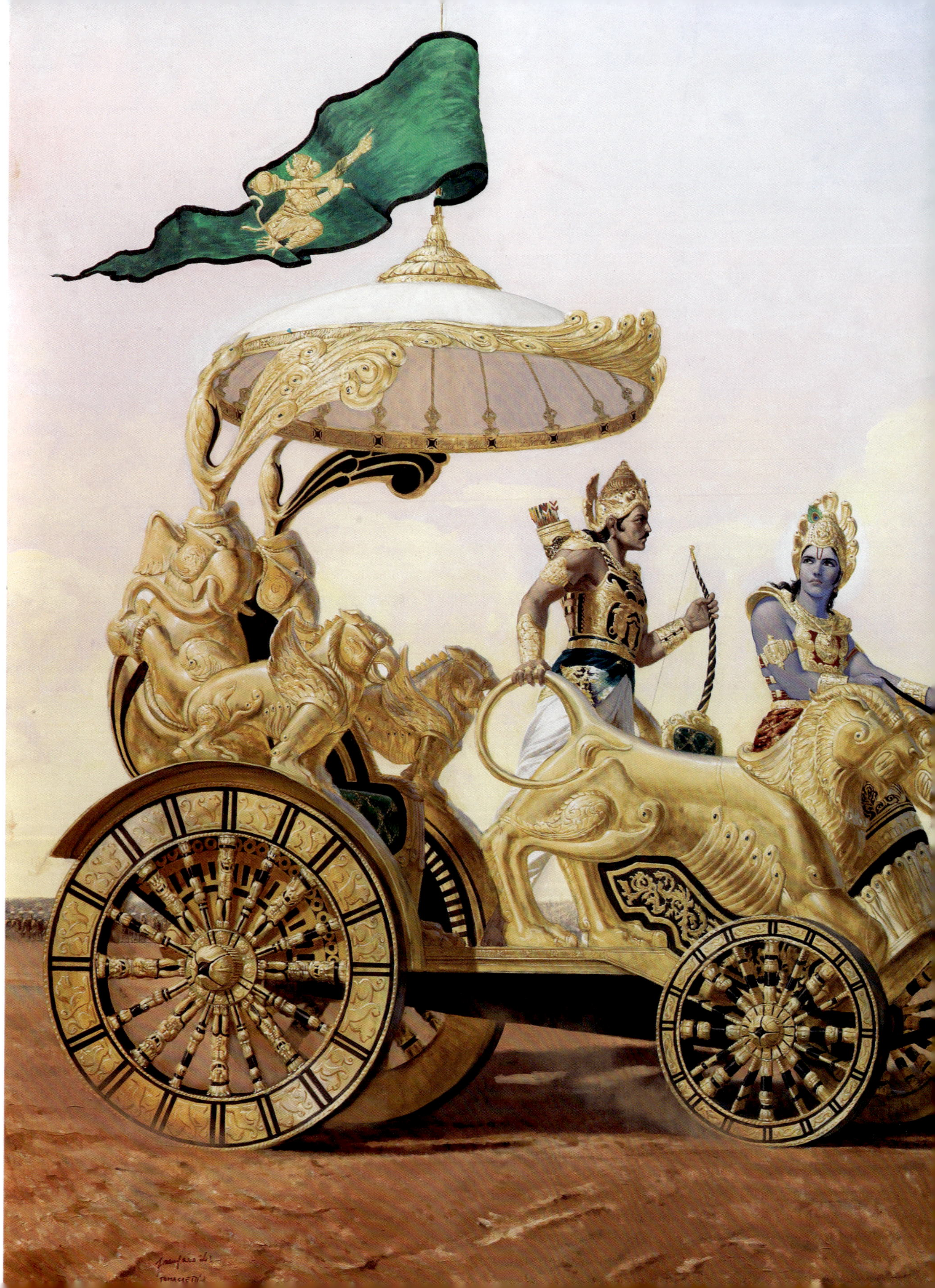

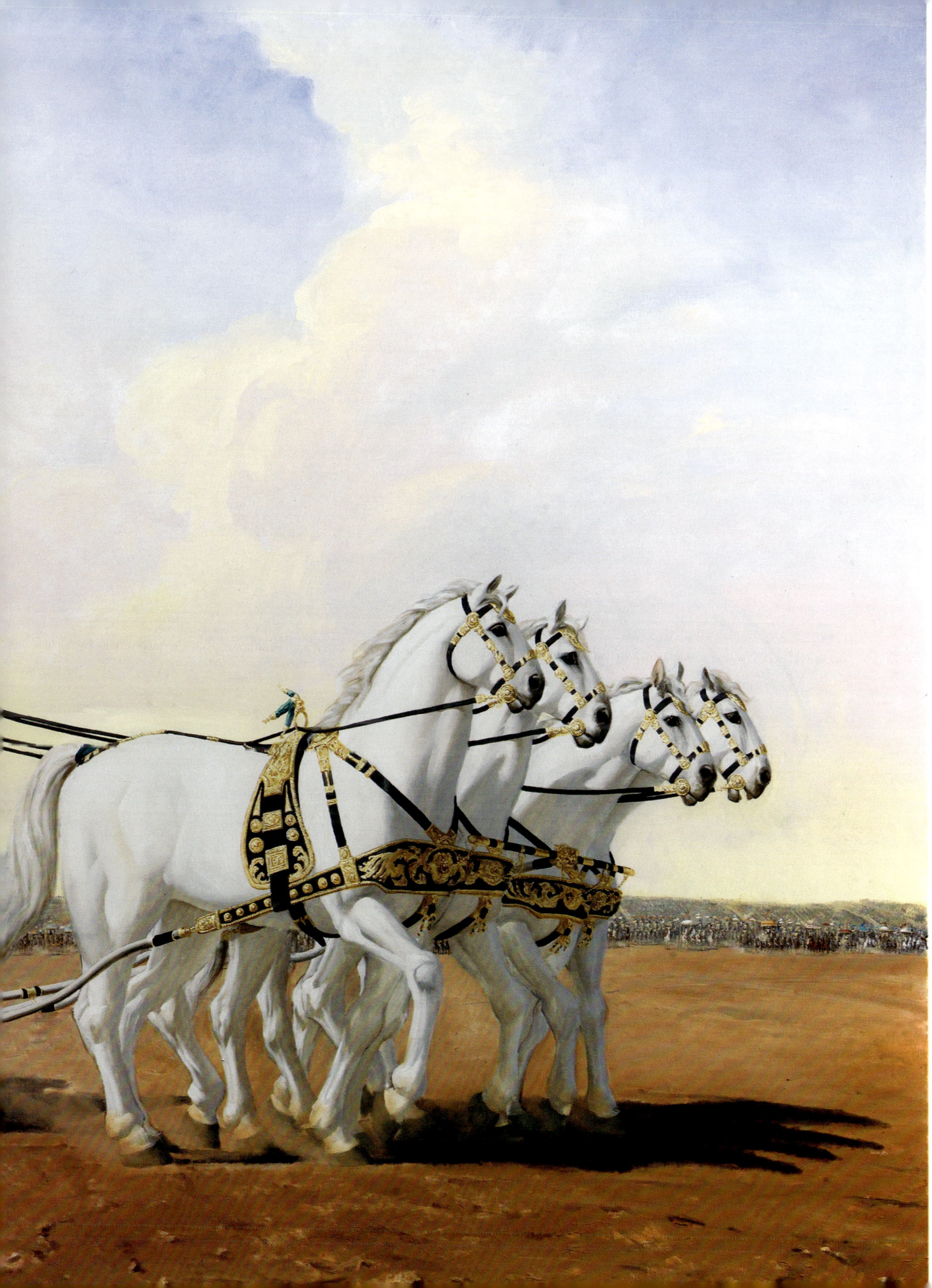

In The Tent

It was the eleventh day of battle. Bhishma had fallen and now Drona was in command. The two armies again faced each another, weapons at the ready. Drona had devised a plan to capture Yudhisthira, knowing that this would end the war there and then. But word had reached the Pandavas and they were closely guarding their leader. Karna, who in a fit of anger against Bhishma had sworn not to fight while he was in command, had finally ridden out into battle. He and Drona bore down fiercely upon their foes, intent on seizing Yudhisthira. But Arjuna was by his side and he fought so powerfully that not even the mighty Drona could get near Yudhisthira. He was driven back by incessant volleys of arrows shot by Arjuna.

The Pandava warrior fired off his deadly shafts so thick and fast from his inexhaustible quiver that he could hardly be seen. Gradually the sun sank below the western horizon and the warriors made their weary way back to camp. After rest and refreshment both sides came together to plan the next day's strategy. In the Kaurava tent there was dismay. Drona knew he could not contain his disciple Arjuna. He said to Duryodhana, "I have told you this before. While Arjuna is by his brother's side I cannot capture him." Drona asked Duryodhana to make some arrangement so that Arjuna would be taken away from Yudhisthira. The Kaurava leader then turned to King Susharma who commanded a great contingent of warriors. "Use your vast forces to distract Arjuna.

Then Drona can seize his brother." Susharma had a history with Arjuna, who had humiliated him on several occasions by defeating him in battle. He immediately agreed. "Yes, I welcome this chance to avenge myself against Arjuna. Tomorrow I will assail him with my fifty thousand chariots. Either he will lie on the battlefield slain by me, or I and all my men will repair to the regions of the gods, slain by him." Susharma made a solemn vow before the sacred fire that he either he or Arjuna would not return alive from the next day's fight. After they had made this plan the Kauravas felt sure that tomorrow they would finally end the war by capturing Yudhisthira. Drona was still doubtful, knowing that the Pandavas had Krishna on their side. He said, "Either we will capture the king, or if not I shall slay one the great heroes in his army. Know this for certain."

On the Pandava's side news of this plan reached them through their spies. They met to discuss their response. Gathered in the tent were the five brothers and Arjuna's disciple Satyaki, as well as his son Abhimanyu. Yudhisthira said, "How shall we deal with this new threat?" Arjuna reassured him, "Do not worry, here is the invincible Satyaki. Even if I am away from you he shall remain by your side. Drona cannot capture you in his presence" Abhimanyu said, "I too shall stand firm in the face of Drona's attack. Have no fear for I am acquainted with all of his manoeuvres." After deciding on the next day's strategy the Pandavas retired for the night, confident that Drona's plan would not succeed.

In The Tent
Oil on Canvas, 175 x 230 cm (pp. 92-93)

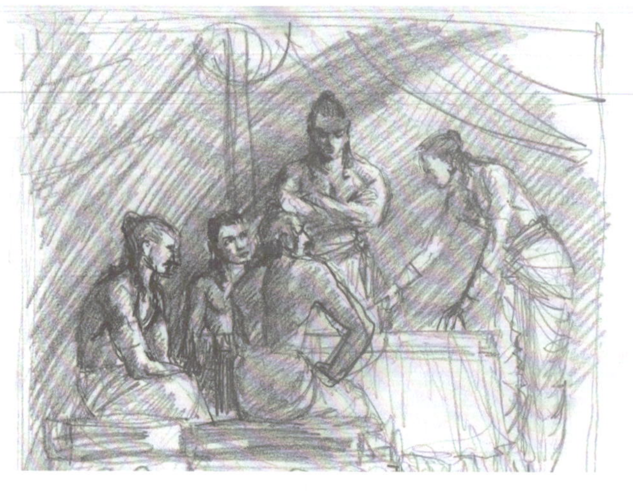

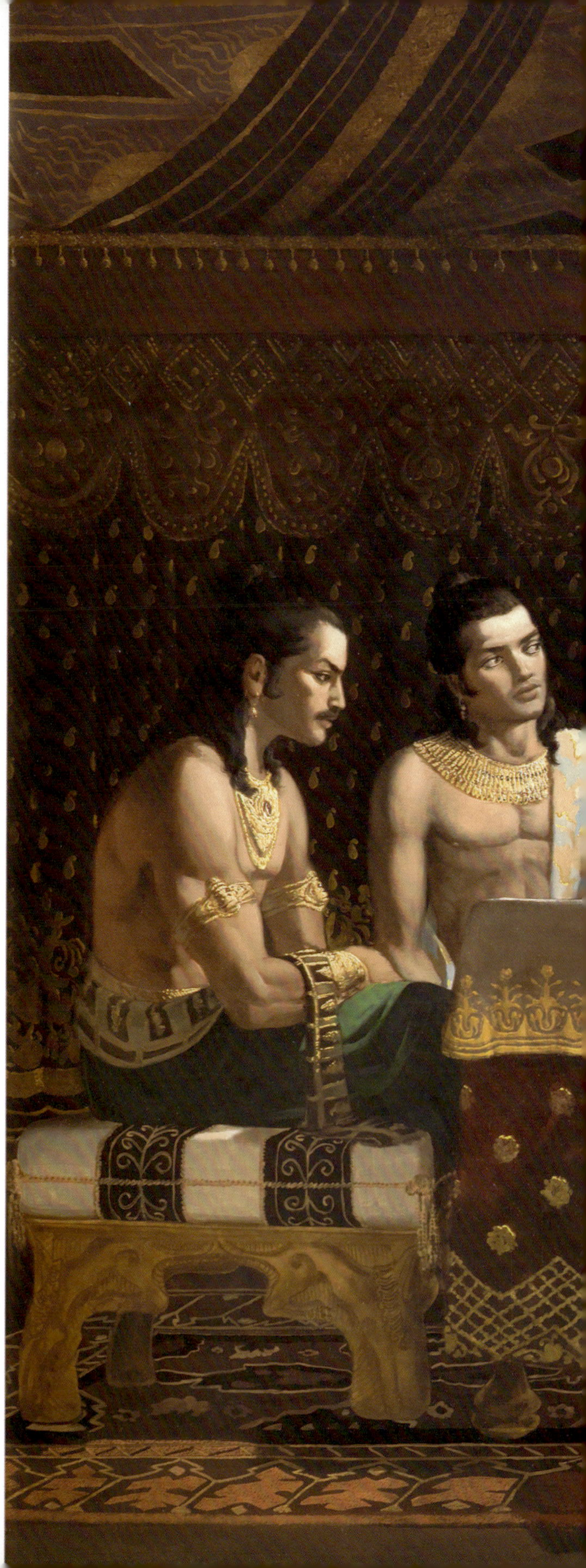

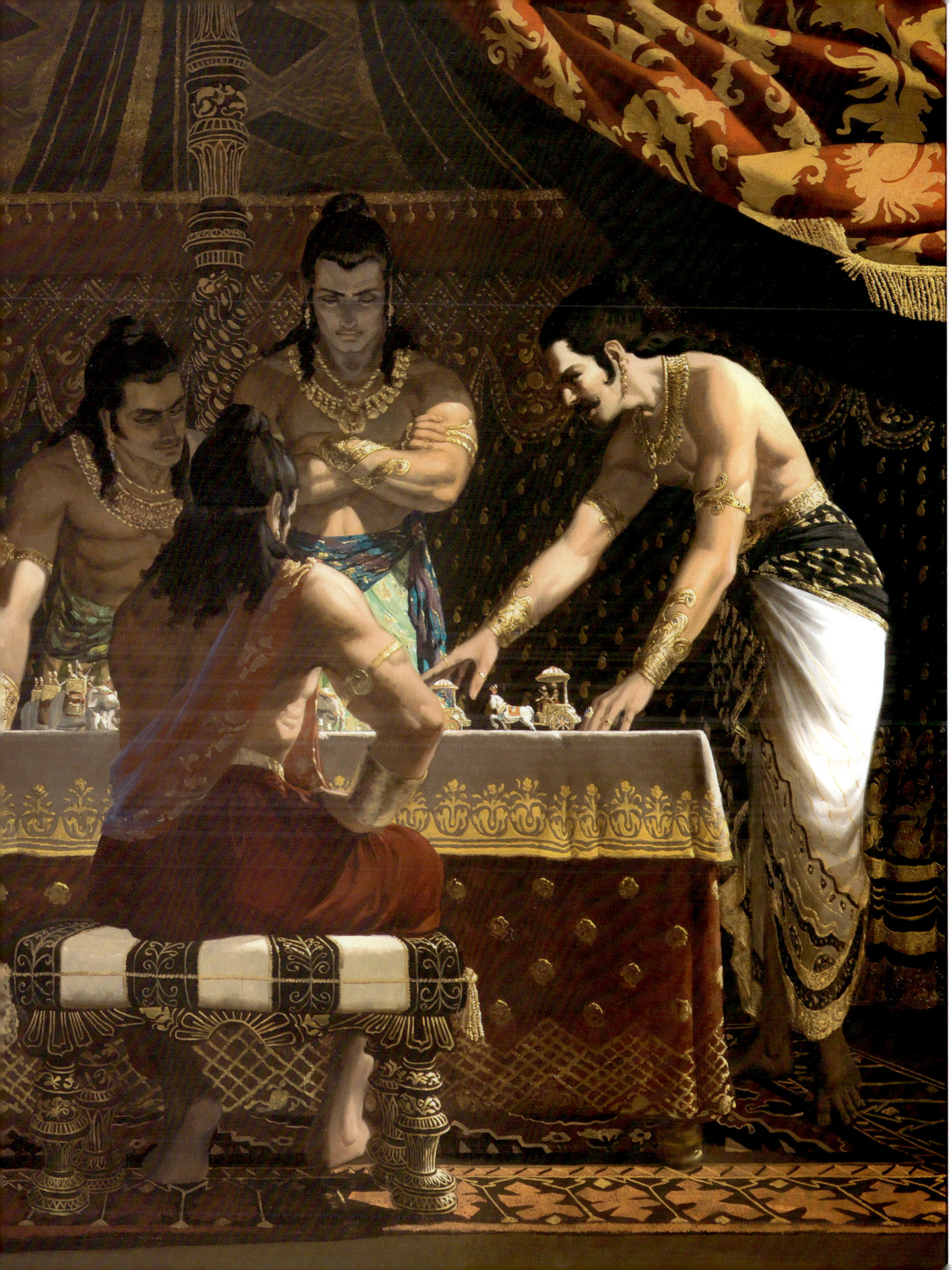

The Young Hero

It was the thirteenth day of the battle. Having just assumed command of the Kaurava forces Drona was intent on bringing a swift end to the war. He planned to capture Yudhisthira, for that would immediately give victory to the Kauravas. Drona knew that while Arjuna was nearby it would be impossible to carry out his plan, so he arranged for him to be engaged on another part of the battlefield. An entire division of warriors thus challenged Arjuna and took him towards the south, while in the north Drona began to arrange his forces in the virtually impenetrable Chakra formation. There were only a few warriors knew the secret of breaking that great array. Among the Pandava fighters only Arjuna and Krishna had that knowledge and they were both far away.

Gradually the Kaurava troops arranged themselves into the complex circular formation and began to advance toward Yudhisthira's position. Drona felt sure that either they would capture the Pandava king, or while attempting to defend him another of the Pandava's heroes would be trapped within the Chakra. Seeing the Chakra, Yudhisthira could at once understand Drona's plan. He knew that none of his warriors except Arjuna could break it open. If not checked it would wreak havoc among his troops. He looked around anxiously and saw Arjuna's son Abhimanyu who he knew had been taught how to enter the array by his father. Yudhisthira called out to him, "My dear Abhimanyu, can you break into this fearsome phalanx?" Abhimanyu said he could, but there was a problem. "I cannot get out array should it close behind me, for I only heard from my father how to enter."

Yudhisthira reassured him that he and his brothers would be right behind him. "We shall smash apart the formation as soon as you enter. Do not be anxious."Abhimanyu stood tall in his chariot. Although just sixteen years old he was equal to his father in prowess and knew no fear in battle. In a loud and heroic voice he declared, "For the pleasure of my father and uncles I shall today accomplish a terrific deed that will glorify my dynasty. I shall crush the enemy host and enter the Chakra." The young hero charged into the fray, releasing countless arrows at the enemy as he wheeled his chariot back and forth. Behind him came other great fighters and a mighty battle ensued. Abhimanyu skilfully weaved his way between the enemy generals who were stationed at key points in the array. None could stop him as he pressed forward.

His stream of arrows cut down warriors on all sides. He overcame all the great Kaurava heroes who fell back stunned from his attack. Even Drona himself could not resist him. Soon he was in the midst of the Chakra and he looked back to see if his uncles were behind him. However, they had been stopped by Jayadratha who had been given a boon by Shiva that he would be able to once defeat each of the Pandavas. Hence they had not been able to get past him and could only watch helplessly as Abhimanyu was enveloped by the Kaurava forces. In the midst of many thousands of warriors Abhimanyu did not flinch in the least. He span in his chariot with his bow constantly drawn to a circle. It seemed as if his was firing arrows in all directions simultaneously. No one could approach him. Chariots, horses, elephants and slain warriors lay everywhere.

More and more warriors tried to close around him and check his progress, but he could not be stopped. The enemy forces were dispersed like leaves blown in the wind. Duryodhana became infuriated. "How has this mere boy defeated all our fighters? Watch now as I punish him." He rushed at Abhi-

M. vol IV pag. 58 / DRONA PARVA

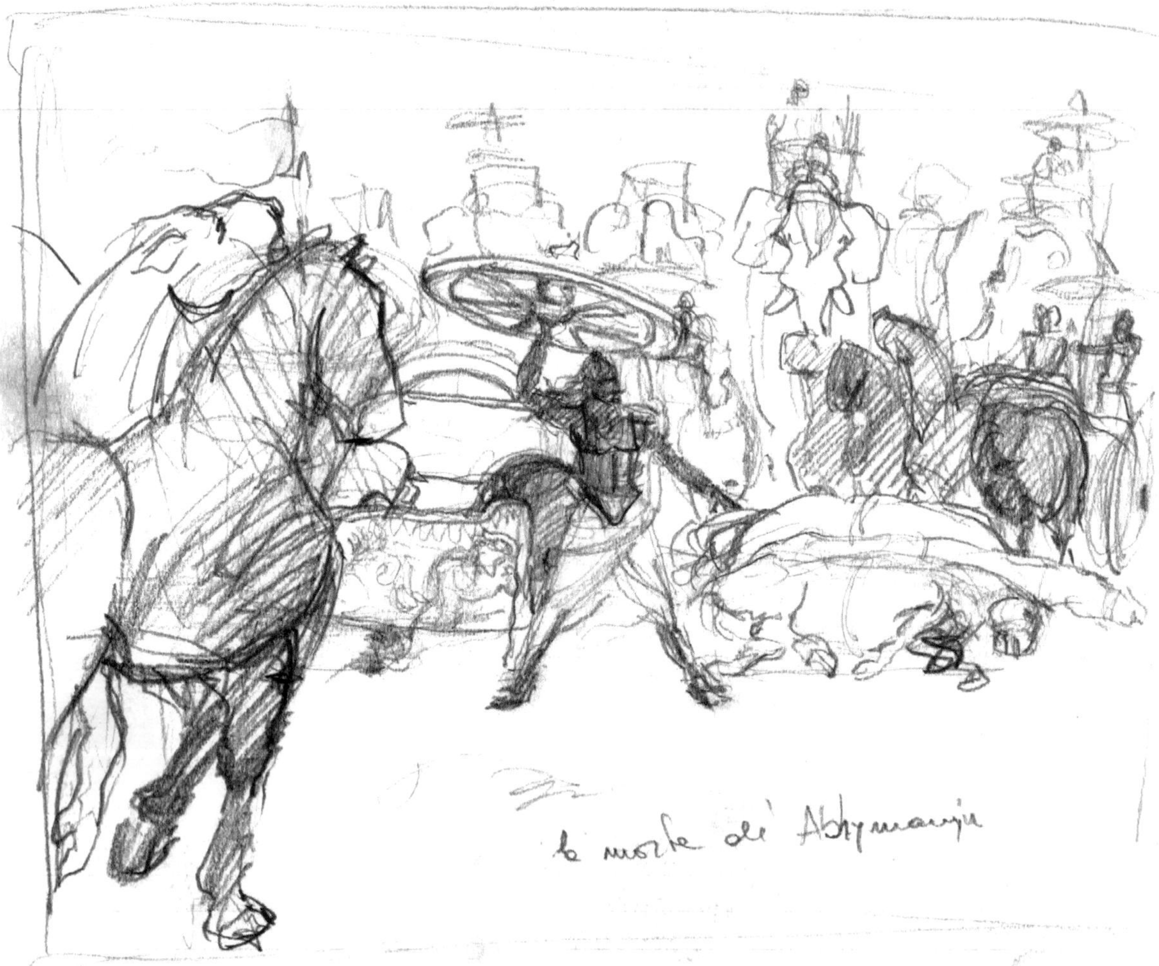

manyu who immediately turned to face him. He shot a mighty arrow that sent Duryodhana reeling in his chariot and Drona rushed to his rescue. The Kaurava commander was filled with admiration for Arjuna's son. The boy was truly as great as his father. It would take the combined efforts of his best fighters to stop him from destroying the whole Kaurava army. Calling them together, Drona gave orders to Karna, Kripa, Ashvatthama, Duryodhana and Kritavarman. They would attack the boy from all sides and render him helpless. It would not be a fair fight, but Drona saw no option.

The Kauravas began to execute their heinous plan. Attacking Abhimanyu from the front, back and sides they smashed apart his chariot, slew his horses and shattered his weapons and armour. The boy leapt down without any fear and continued fighting with his sword and shield, slaying still more warriors. But gradually the six great fighters closed around him and disarmed him with their arrows. Still the dauntless youth fought on, taking up a chariot wheel and whirling it above his head. When that was cut to pieces he picked up a club and killed dozens more soldiers who dared come near him. At last Dushasana's son Durmashana took up his mace and challenged him. They fought for some time and suddenly brought down their heavy maces on each other at the same time. Both dropped to the earth, but Durmashana rose up before the fatigued Abhimanyu came to his senses. He brought his mace down onto Abhimanyu head with all his power and the boy finally fell dead.

The Young Hero
Oil on Canvas, 150 x 350 cm (pp. 98-99)

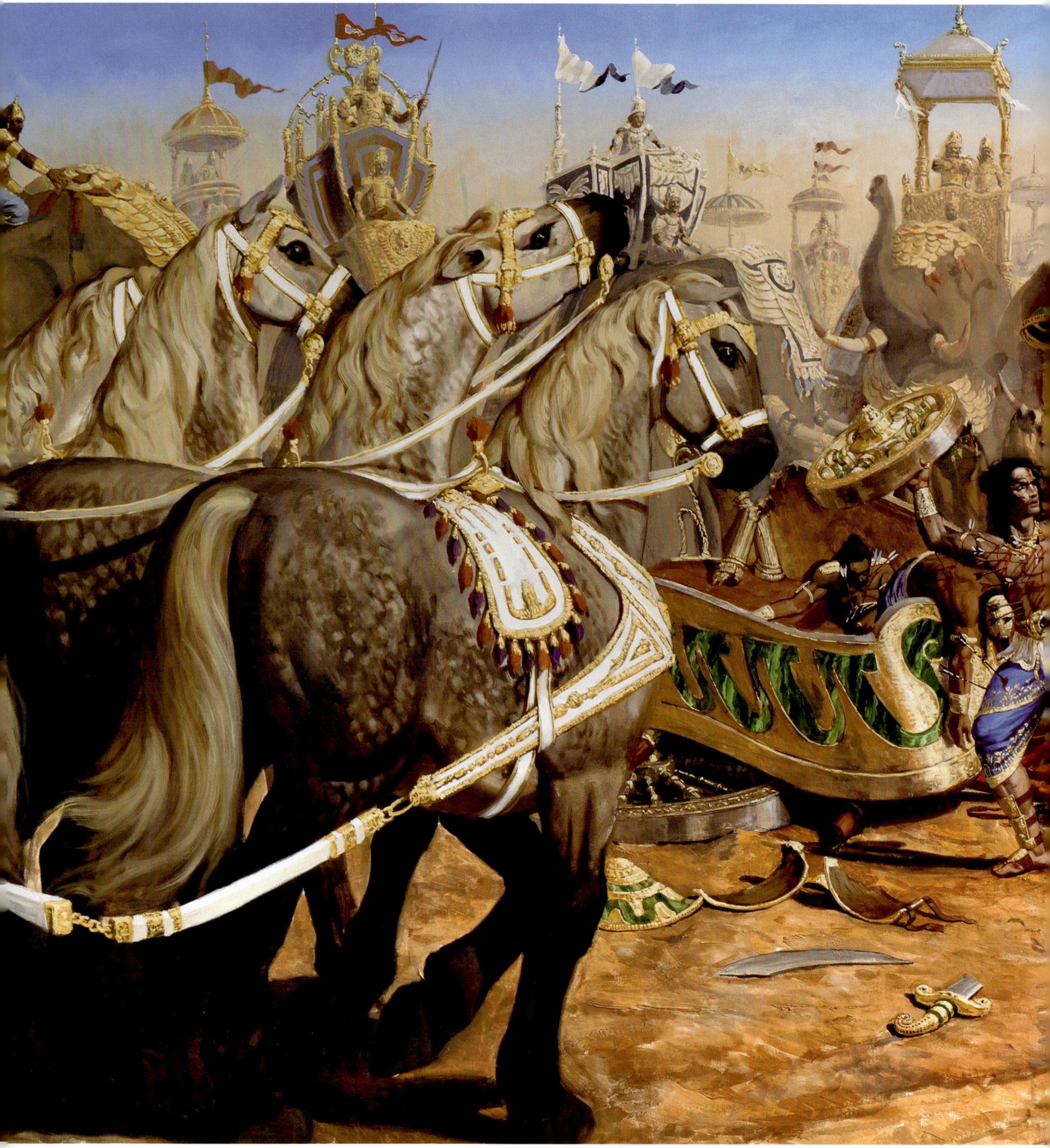

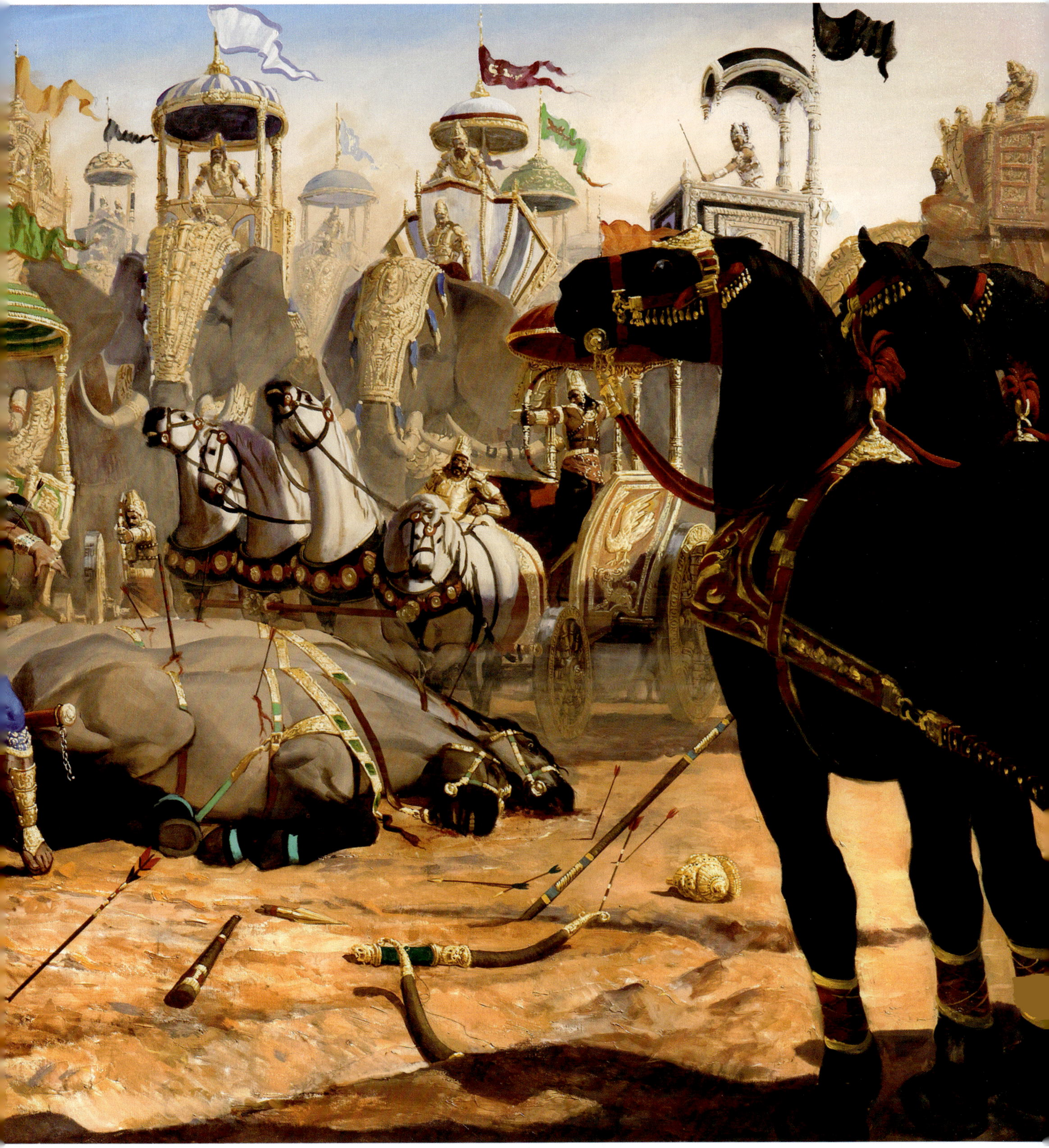

Bhima and Bhagadatta

The sun rose upon the eighth day of the battle of Kurukshetra. Once again the two armies charged upon each other and a ferocious conflict ensued raising the hairs on the body of all observers. Arrows flew in all directions severing arms, legs and heads. A terrific and deafening noise filled the earth and sky as fighters roared their battle cries, horses whinnied, elephants trumpeted and countless bow strings twanged. Mangled bodies of men and were strewn everywhere and it was difficult to move across the battlefield.

Riding in his massive chariot Bhima raced into the melee intent on killing the hundred sons of Dhritarastra. He had made this vow and was setting about fulfilling it with grim determination. Coming across a group of the brothers he licked his lips and drew his bowstring back to his ear. With four yard long shafts he cut off the heads of four of the Kaurava princes in a matter of moments. The others rallied and attacked the Pandava, shrouding him in a great cloud of arrows. Undaunted by this attack Bhima emerged from the web of arrows and swiftly slew two more of the brothers.

Seeing this Duryodhana called out for assistance in checking the rampaging Bhima, who immediately turned his attack on the Kaurava leader. He fired a cluster of arrows that knocked Duryodhana off balance and made him spin round in his chariot, dazed and confused. A barbarian king named Anga seated on the back of a huge elephant charged into the fray intent on saving Duryodhana. He was followed by a division of other elephants all screaming in fury. Bhima struck Anga's elephant between the eyes with a powerful shaft that stopped it in its tracks. With four more arrows he brought the elephant crashing to the ground.

As it fell like a mountain struck by a thunderbolt, the barbarian chief tried to leap clear; but even as he jumped, Bhima cut off his head with a razor-headed arrow fired with deadly accuracy. Seeing their leader slain, the other elephant warriors fled. Having come back to his senses Duryodhana tried to rally them, but without success. He backed away from the uncheckable Bhima and saw Bhagadatta coming up fast to assist him. The mighty fighter on his invincible elephant Supratika rushed toward Bhima, seeming to fly over the battlefield. Bhima fired his long shafts at the charging beast, but they fell harmlessly from the armour covering its body. Making the earth shake the elephant raced toward Bhima's chariot and crushed it along with its four horses as Bhima threw himself clear.

Supratika reared up again and again, bellowing in fury and turning its head round and round, looking around for Bhima. The Pandava ran beneath the beast and struck it with his bare arms. In pain the elephant whirled around like a potter's wheel. Bhima came out from beneath it and the beast seized him in its trunk. Bhima spun round and freed himself from the twine of the trunk and again hid beneath the screaming animal that was endeavouring to kill him. Yudhisthira saw Bhima and ordered a division of his own elephants to assist him. As Supratika was diverted by the attack of enemy elephants, Bhima saw his chance and he dashed out.

Bhagadatta urged his elephant on and it roared in fury. The massive animal careered forward, crushing chariots, horses and infantrymen. It's frightful screams terrified the soldiers who fled in all directions. Bhima again faced the elephant and released a dozen shafts which simply glanced off its iron armour. Bhagadatta proceeded to attack Bhima with hundreds of arrows that covered him like a cloud. His goaded Supratika forward hoping to crush Bhima. Other Pandava warriors came up to check the beast with a fierce volley of weapons.

Struck by dozens of arrows Bhagadatta, with blood trickling down his body, seemed like a mass of clouds tinged with the rays of the setting sun.

Taking up a great spear he hurled it with all his power and it struck Bhima full on the breast, knocking him backwards. The mighty Pandava dropped down in a swoon and Bhagadatta let out a great roar of triumph. Hearing that cry and seeing his father in difficulty, the Rakshasa Ghatotkacha rushed to his assistance. He launched a fierce assault on Bhagadatta and drove him back as Bhima returned to his senses. He pulled the lance from his chest and leapt to his feet. Undaunted he ran back into the fray, his whirling mace crushing everything in his path. Gradually the sun set and the troops were withdrawn for the night.

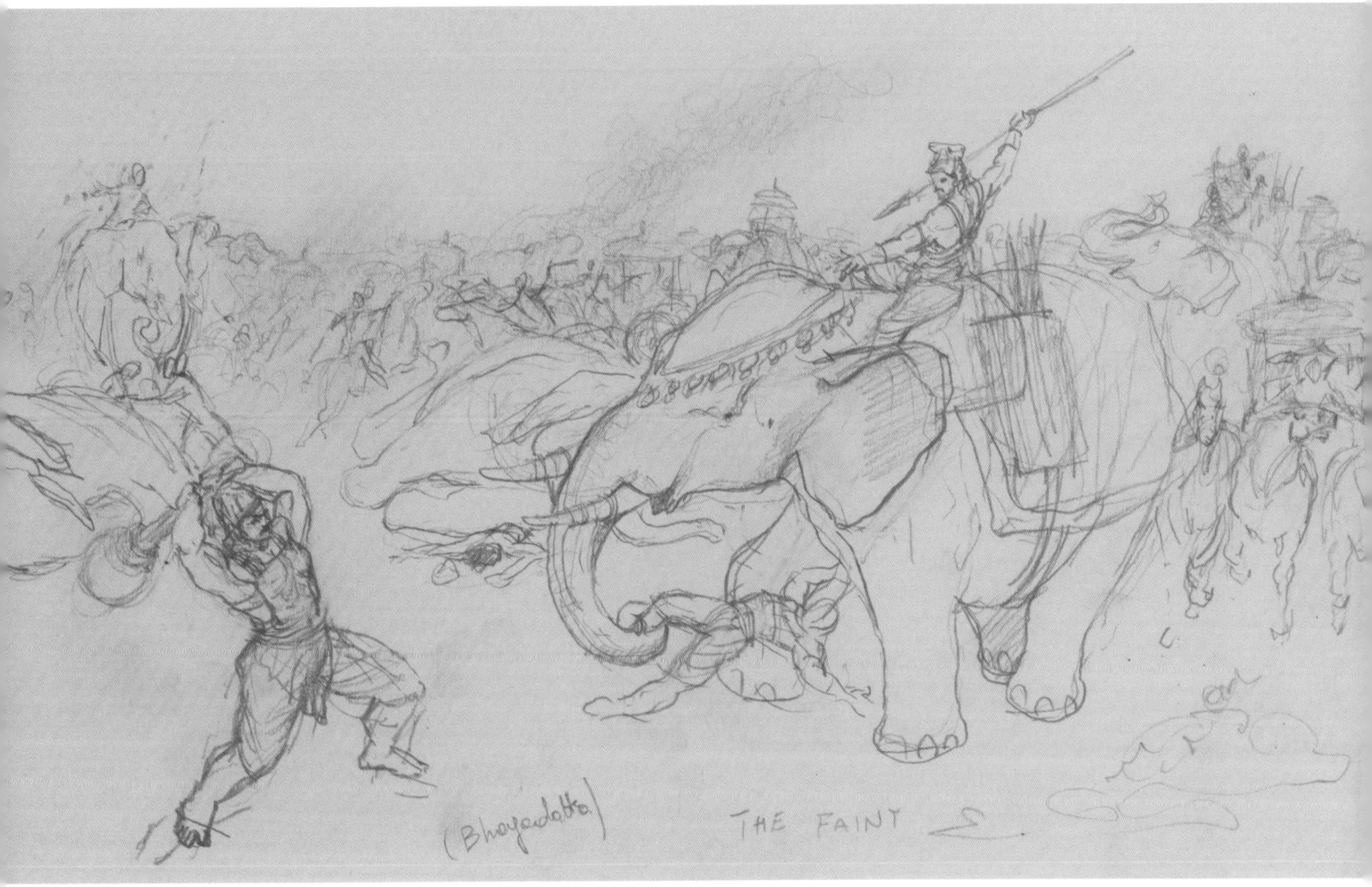

Bhima and Bhagadatta
Oil on Canvas, 200 x 300 cm (pp. 104-105)

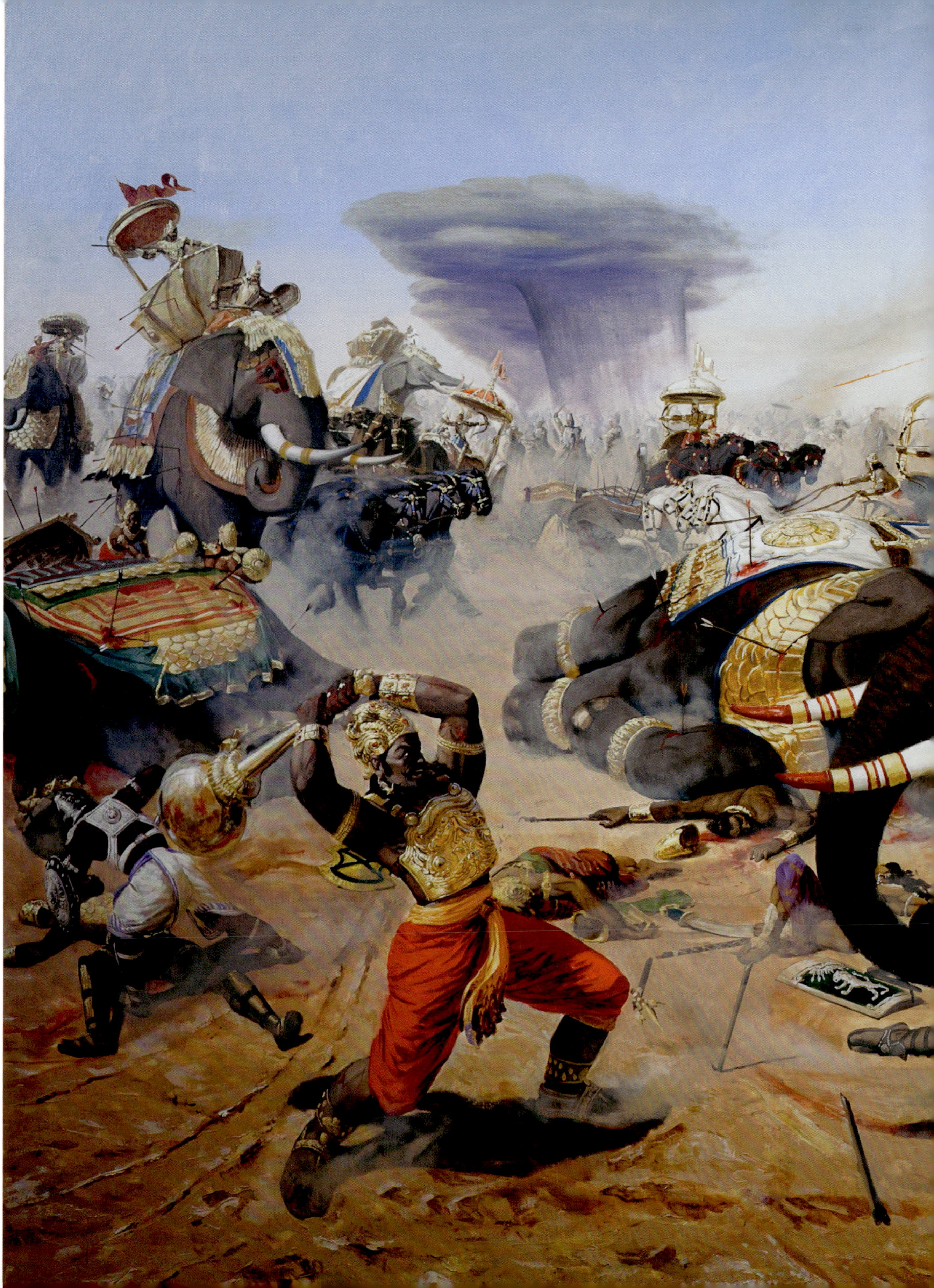

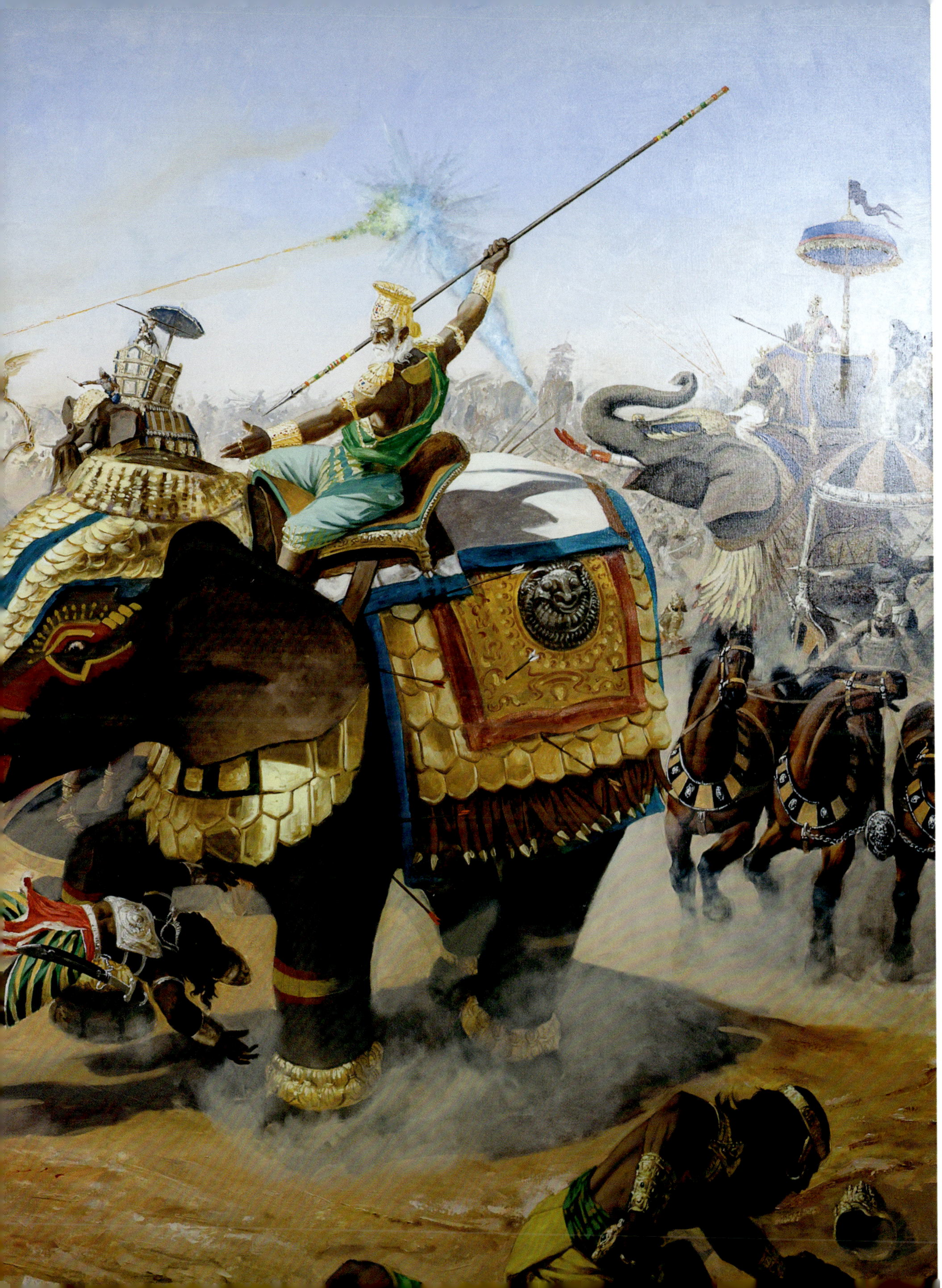

The Fall of the Hero

Bhishma had never wanted to fight against the Pandavas. Repeatedly he had advised Duryodhana and his blind father Dhritarastra that it would be suicidal to oppose the godly brothers. They were supported by Krishna, the Supreme Personality of Godhead. Although not fighting, Krishna's mere presence on the side of the Pandavas would ensure their victory. Bhishma had therefore repeatedly urged Duryodhana to give the Pandavas their rightful share of the kingdom when they emerged from exile.

The old hero's words had fallen on deaf ears. Duryodhana mocked him and Dhritarastra did nothing to check his avaricious son. War could not be averted and when it arrived Bhishma felt an obligation to fight for the Kauravas. They had always maintained him and he had vowed to protect the incumbent monarch in Hastinapura. So it was that Bhishma became the commander-in-chief of the Kaurava forces.

Although the Pandavas loved him like a father, they knew that he was impossible to overcome in battle. Therefore when at last the two great armies were arrayed for battle, Yudhisthira went before Bhishma and said, "Dear Grandfather, I beg your permission to fight you. Please give me your blessings. Tell me how we shall be able to defeat you in this war." Bhishma shed tears of affection for the humble Pandava king. He got down and blessed Yudhisthira, saying, "There is no warrior anywhere who can conquer me, not even the king of the gods. Ask me again at a later time and I shall tell you how I may be slain."

From the outset of battle Bhishma displayed his incomparable power. Riding out on his great silver chariot he began to cut swathes through the opposing army. With his bow always drawn to a circle he shot his arrows so swiftly that they appeared to fly in an endless line. No one could even approach him in the fight. As soon as any warrior came near they were cut to pieces by his relentless volleys of arrows. Defying his advanced age, the great hero seemed to dance in his chariot as he fought. With a single long shaft he would slay three of four men seated on an elephant. Then with another he would kill the elephant itself. He shattered chariots and slew the warriors within them with steel pointed shafts that never missed their target. All the soldiers opposing him fled for their lives. No one could even look at him as he pressed forward. It seemed as if he had multiplied himself into numerous forms. His arrows appeared to be flying in all directions at once. Cries went up from the afflicted warriors he attacked. "Help! Save us from Bhishma!" Gradually the sun set and the Pandava army was spared further misery at Bhishma's hands.

The two armies withdrew for the night and Yudhisthira consulted with Krishna. "How shall we stop Bhishma? Surely he will destroy us all." Krishna reminded Yudhisthira that Bhishma had said to ask him how he could be overcome. "That time has come. Go to him now." Yudhisthira went at once with all his brothers to Bhishma's tent and fell before him. With tears in his eyes he said, "My lord, pray tell us how we can defeat you. I fear that you will annihilate my entire army." Bhishma said, "Dear child, know that when I stand with weapons in hand I cannot be overpowered by men or gods. Only when I lower my weapons can that happen. Here is my vow."

The old warrior said that he would not fight with a female, and that one of Yudhisthira's fighters, Sikandhi, had been a woman named Amba in his past life. She had felt mistreated by Bhishma and by the power of the rishis whom she had beseeched she had taken birth as a man in this life to kill him. Bhishma said, "Place Sikandhi at the front of the battle and have Arjuna stand behind him. Only his or Krishna's arrows can bring me down." The idea of killing Bhishma filled all five brothers with sorrow. He had practically taken the place of their father Pandu after his death. With heavy hearts they made their way back to their camp.

The Rush of the Hero
Oil on Canvas, 70 x 100 cm (pp. 110-111)

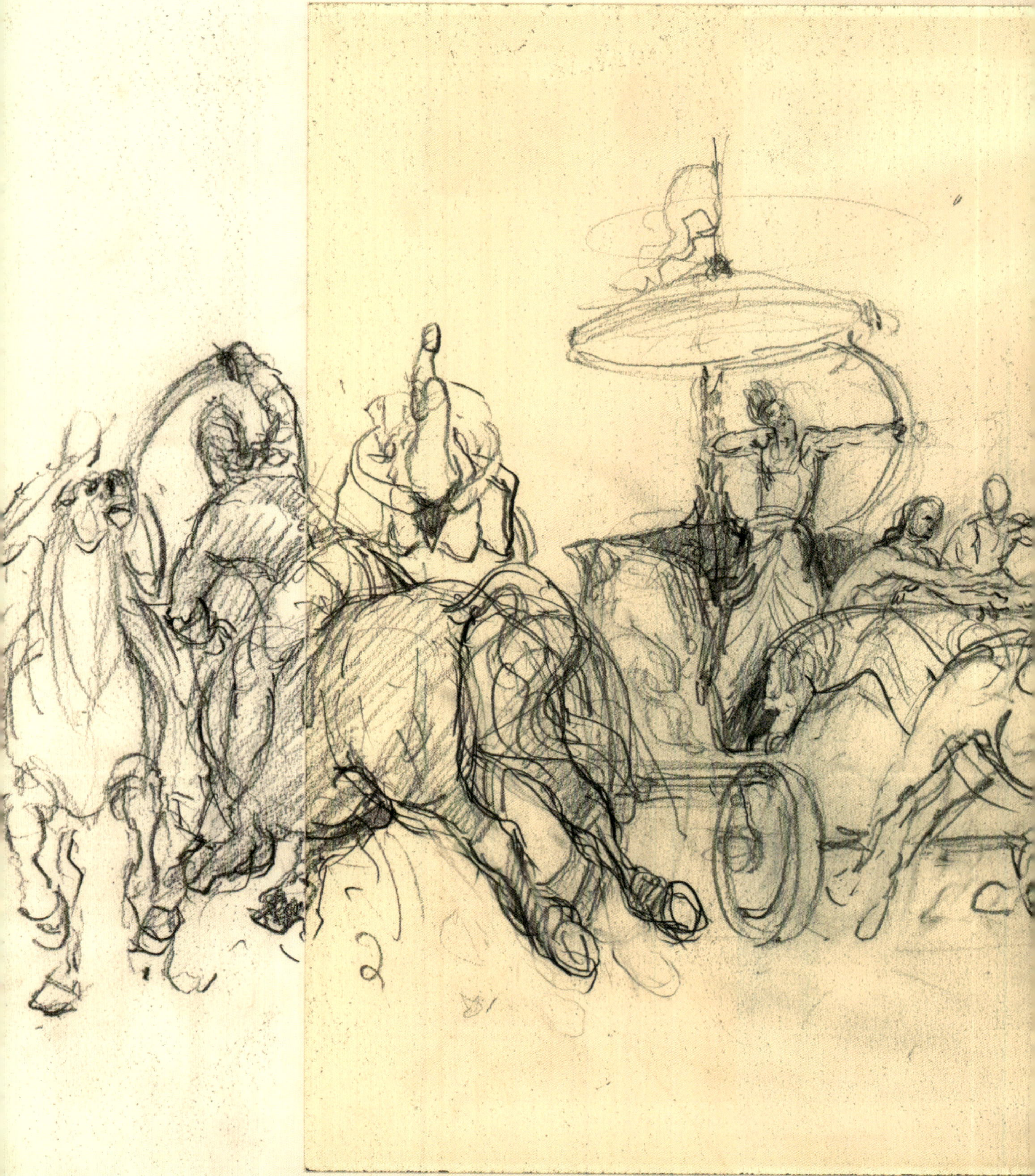

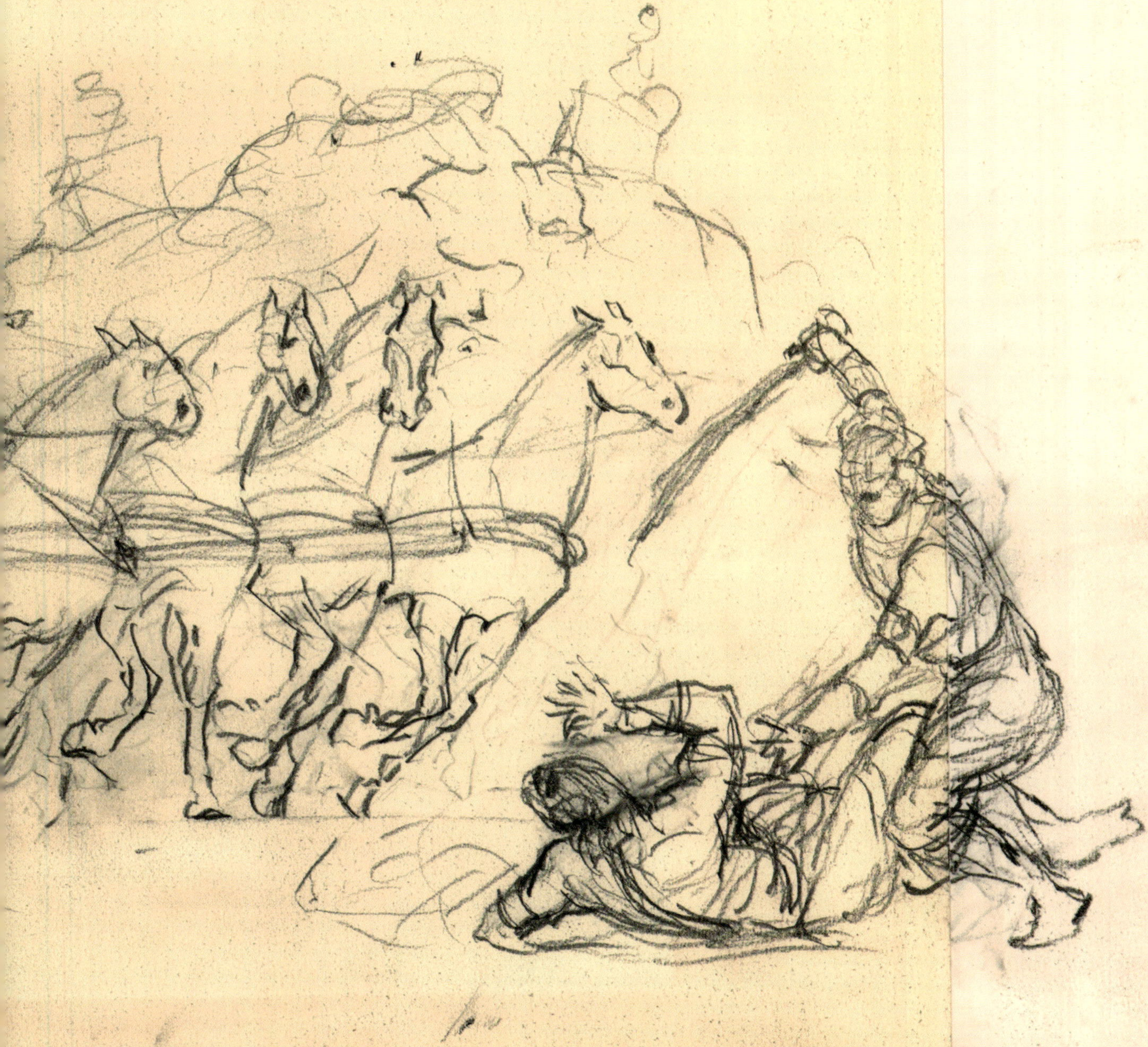

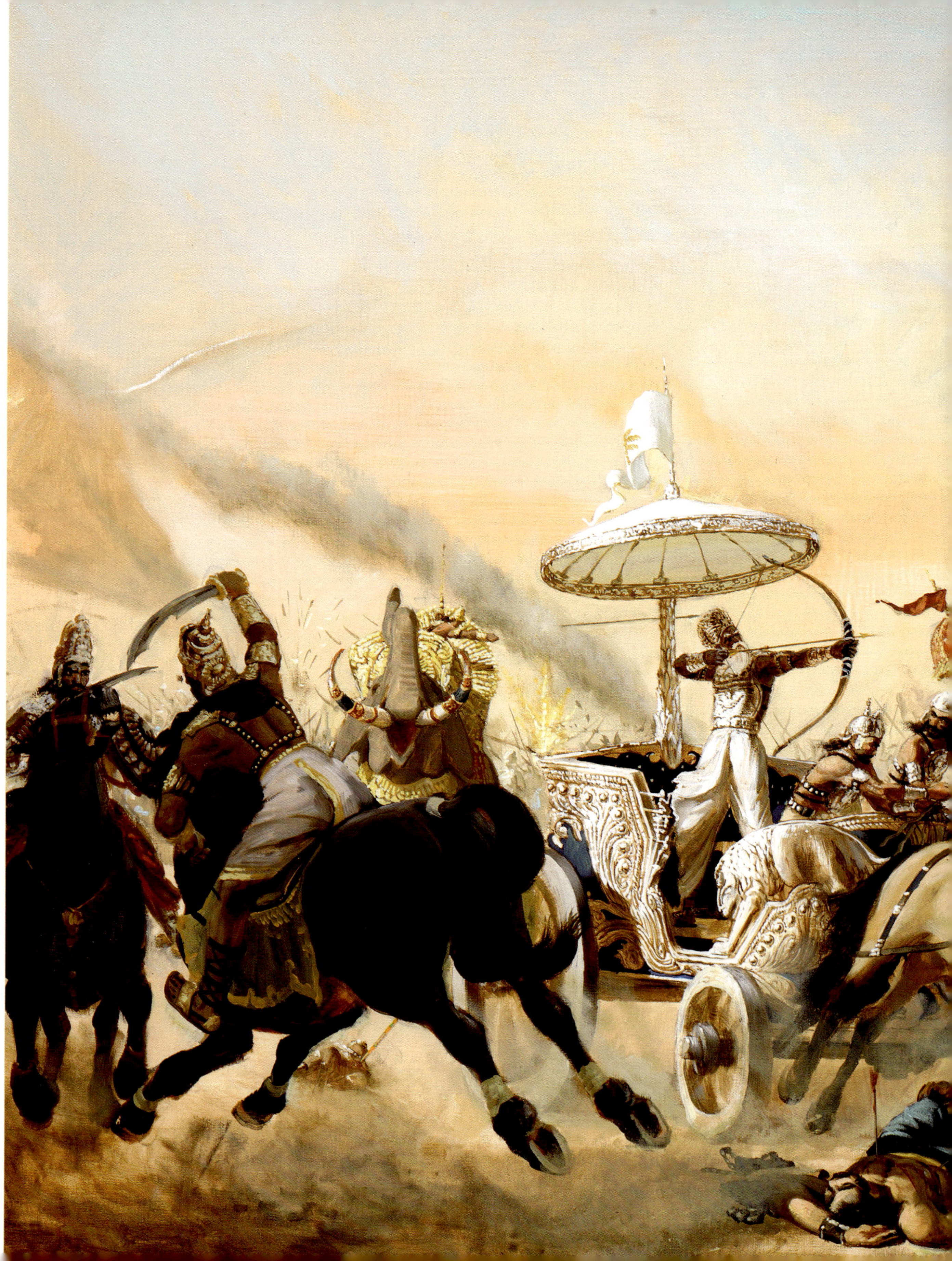

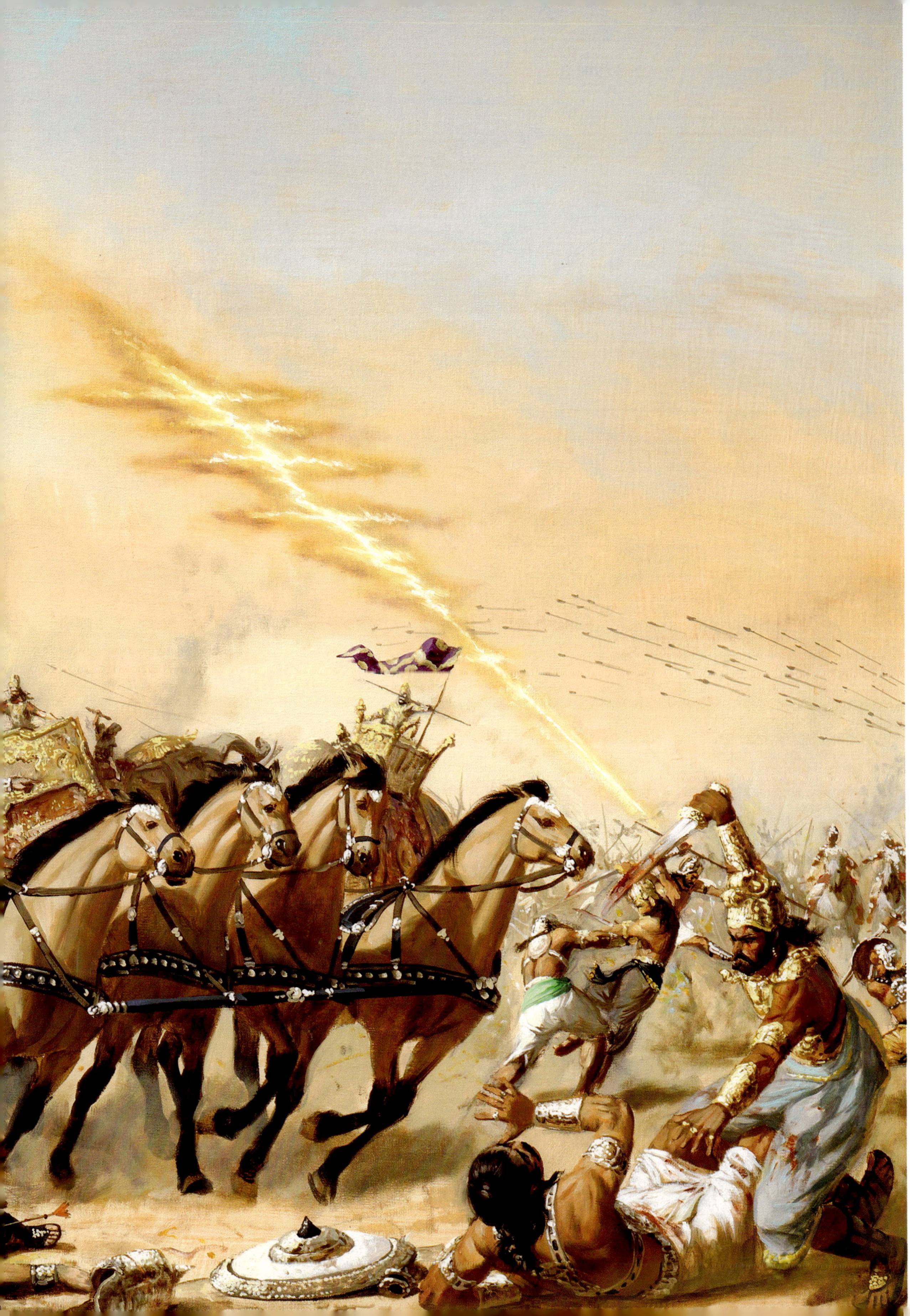

The next day the battle began as it had left off the day before, with Bhishma wreaking havoc. He continued fighting to his full power creating still more carnage among the Pandava army. Knowing his time was near he exerted himself with a final supreme effort. Like a fire consuming a forest he destroyed the Pandava troops in their thousands. Sikandhi gradually came to the fore of the battle and positioned himself in front of Bhishma. Remembering his former enmity he called out a challenge and fired his arrows at him. Bhishma called back, "I shall not fight with you Sikandhi, for I consider you to be Amba."

Bhishma turned away from Sikandhi and continued his assault as other Kauravas came to protect him. Arjuna came up to Sikandhi and said, "Do not fear. I shall support you and deal with all these warriors . Attack the grandfather again." Sikandhi again shot arrows at Bhishma but still he would not retaliate. Arjuna kept up a fierce attack on the other Kauravas, beating them back until he faced Bhishma alone. With Sikandhi by his side he pressed forward and attacked his implacable foe. Bhishma fought back, striking Arjuna with many arrows. The two mighty heroes waged a terrific fight that made all onlookers gasp in amazement.

Suddenly from the heavens Bhishma heard a celestial voice telling him that it was time for him to desist from battle. "Put down your weapons, for the

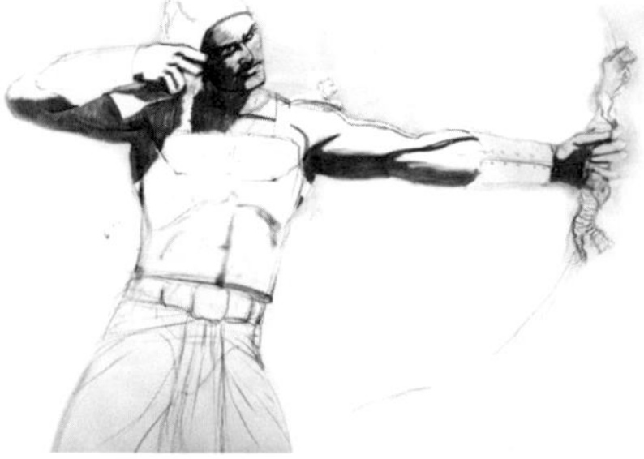

Shoot Him Now
Oil on Canvas, 300 x 200 cm (p. 114)

moment ordained for your end is approaching." Bhishma looked over at Arjuna. He saw that Sikandhi was again in front of him, calling out his challenges and firing at him. Slowly the great Kuru general lowered his bow. Urged on by Krishna, Arjuna maintained a relentless assault. He shot clusters of arrows that began to pierce Bhishma's body. Standing by his side was Dushashana, and Bhishma said to him, "These arrows piercing me can only be from Arjuna. They are each like Indra's thunderbolt weapon.

Those fired by Sikandhi surely could not harm me." So many arrows struck Bhishma that there was not even two fingers space on his body that was not pierced. The arrows protruded from him in hundreds. As the horrified Kauravas looked on he slowly toppled from his chariot and fell to the ground. Landing on his back he was completely supported by the arrows, his body not touching the ground. A great cry of anguish went up from the Kauravas. "Bhishma is slain!" Hearing this Bhishma said, "I am still living. The time for my death has not yet arrived."

Bhishma had been blessed by his father Shantanu that he could choose the moment that he left his body. Resting on his bed of arrows, he waited for that auspicious moment as all the great warriors from both sides came up to pay him their respects. Yudhisthira was filled with both relief and grief. His most powerful opponent was laid low, but he still loved him like a father. How terrible was the life of a warrior.

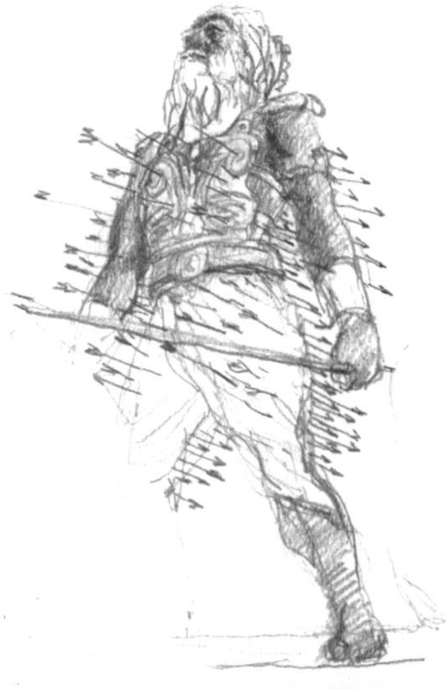

The Fall of the Hero
Oil on Canvas, 200 x 150 cm (p. 115)

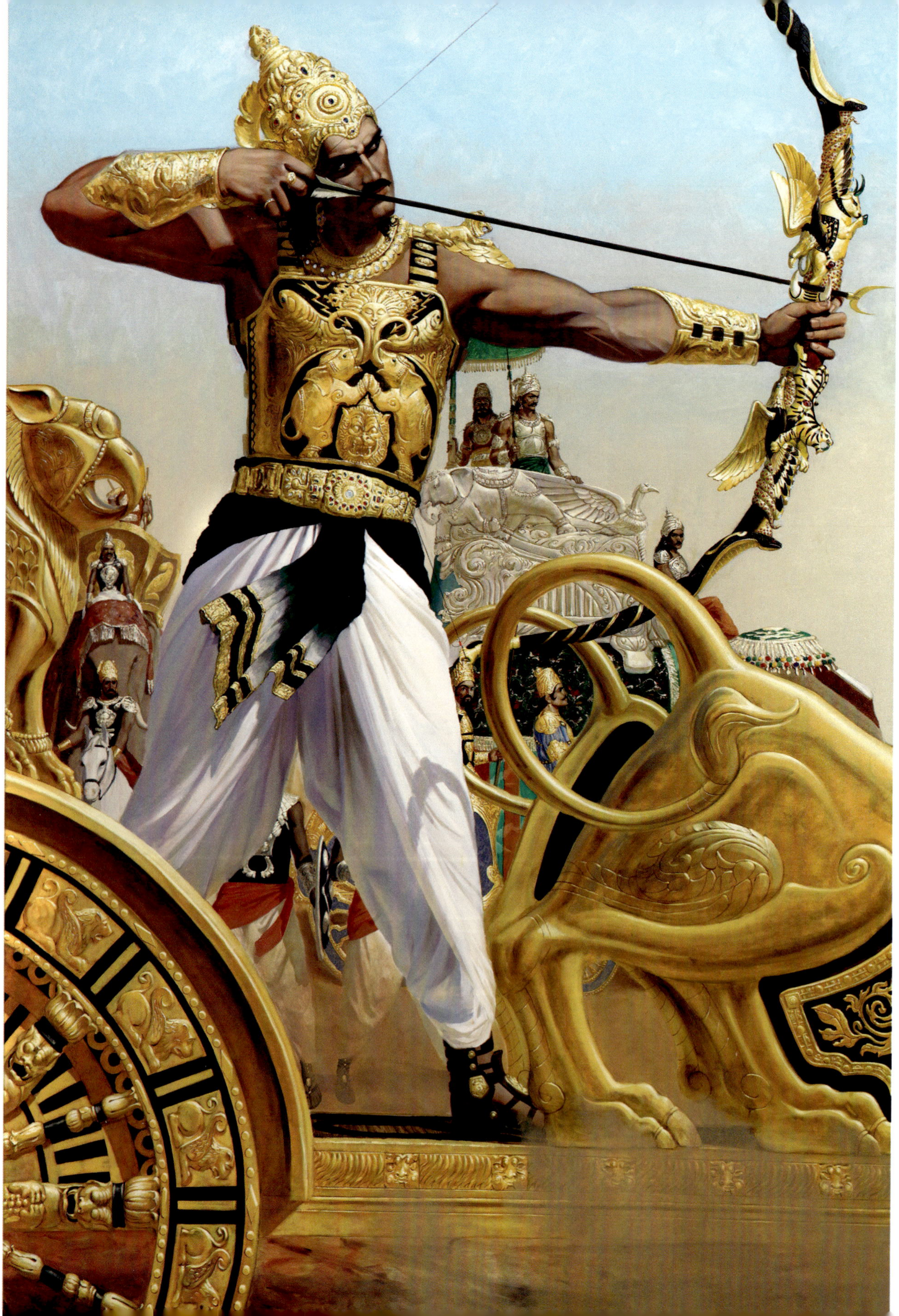

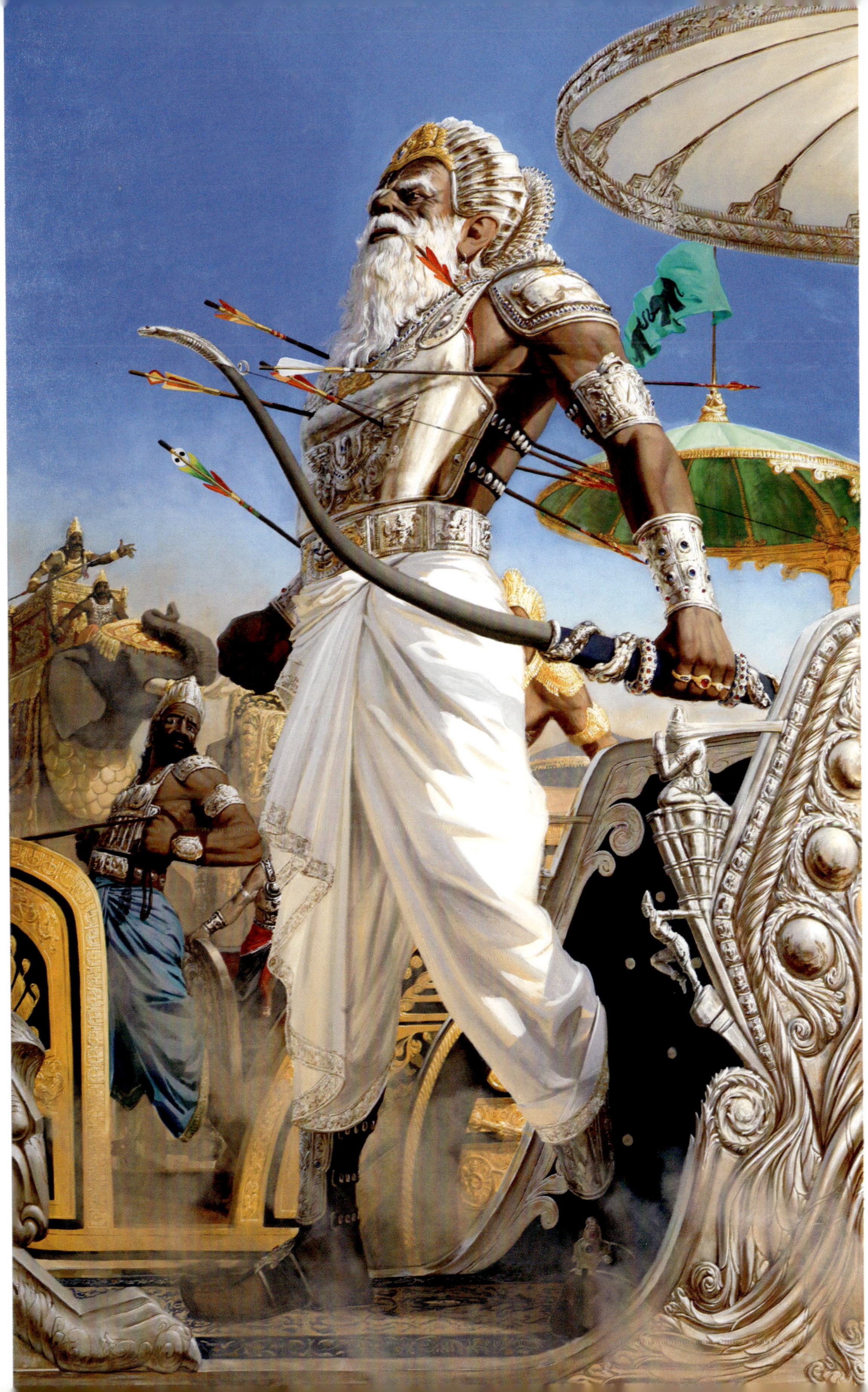

Karna

For seventeen days the battle had been raging. Gradually the Pandavas had gained the upper hand over their foes, the Kauravas. Most of the great Kaurava heroes had been slain, but perhaps the greatest among them, Karna, still survived. So too did his lifelong sworn enemy, Arjuna. The time had come for the final confrontation between these two invincible fighters.

On this fateful day one of them would not be returning to his camp. The brilliant golden chariots of the two heroes came together like the meeting of two suns. Like the king of the gods Indra encountering the demon chief Bali, they approached one another for their deadly battle. Everyone stopped fighting in order to watch them. Thousands of drums and trumpets sounded along with countless conch shells creating a deafening din.

The fight began with a flurry of fierce arrows fired by both warriors. Colliding in the sky those steel pointed shafts gave off showers of sparks. The sky was covered with great clouds of arrows, creating a dark shadow across the battlefield. The two roaring warriors countered each other's attacks, like the east and west wind struggling together. Striking down each other's arrows as they rained down upon them, the mighty combatants seemed like the sun and moon emerging from storm clouds. Both men employed celestial weapons that brought fearful clusters of blazing missiles onto the battlefield. Their brilliance brightly illuminated all sides blinding those who looked on. Many thousands of warriors were slain by those attacks and they lay here and there in bloodstained and smoking heaps.

Sometimes it seemed that Karna had the advantage, and then Arjuna gained the upper hand. Neither gave any quarter and the stream of arrows and other weapons flying back and forth was incessant. All of a sudden as the battle raged Karna saw with horror that his chariot wheel was slowly sinking into the earth. He recalled how long ago a Brahmin, whose cow he had accidentally slain, had cursed him. "Hear my words," the Brahmin had angrily said. "When you meet your deadliest enemy in battle the earth shall swallow your chariot wheel." That curse was now taking effect.

The chariot came to a halt and Karna looked across at Arjuna, who began to press home his advantage over his stricken foe. Arrows came down upon him even more fiercely as Karna leapt down from the chariot. Taking hold of the wheel he heaved with all his might. His two massive arms looked like a pair of oak trees rising from the earth. Sweat streamed down his face as he exerted himself to his full power, but the wheel would not budge even an inch.

Karna called across to Arjuna, "Wait! Give me one moment to free my wheel. Do not disregard morality and the rules of fair combat by attacking a disabled foe." On Arjuna's chariot Krishna smiled. He came closer to Karna and said, "It is good that you think now of morality, Karna. I wish though you had remembered it on the day you shamed Draupadi by ordering her to be stripped naked in the public assembly. Or on the day you colluded with Duryodhana to kill the Pandavas by arson. Where too was this fine morality when joined with six other mighty warriors to kill the unarmed boy Abhimanyu?"

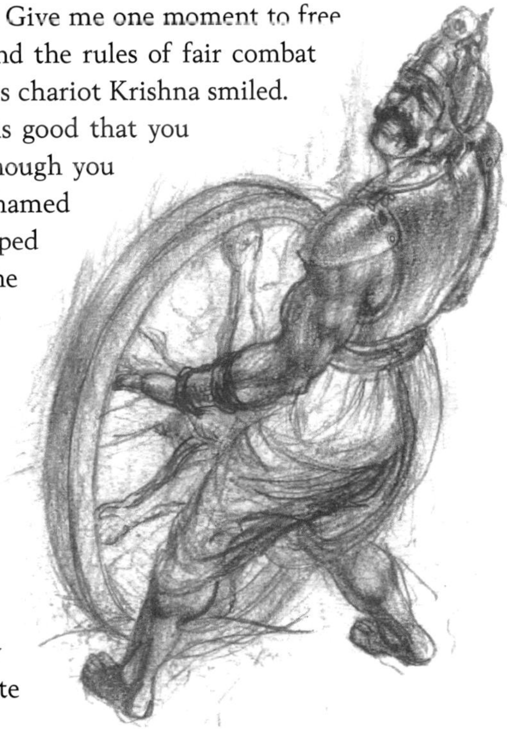

Krishna urged Arjuna not to let up his attack. Karna vaulted back up onto his chariot and discharged a great volley of shafts towards his indomitable enemy. Arjuna was momentarily stunned by the force of Karna's desperate assault. Seeing this Karna once more jumped down and seized hold of the wheel. With a tremendous cry he pulled with all his power. The very earth seemed to rise up with her mountains and seas but the wheel would not be dislodged. Karna wept in frustration, remembering the fateful day his careless arrows had killed the Brahmin's cow.

Krishna said to Arjuna, "Do not delay any longer. Kill him now. Use your most powerful weapon and take his life before he attacks again. A desperate foe is dangerous indeed." Arjuna placed a golden arrow upon his bow and, composing his mind, remembered the ancient mantras to invoke the weapon of Lord Brahma, the greatest of the gods. As he began the incantation he took careful aim at the still struggling Karna. Finishing the prayer he released the arrow and it shrieked through the air like inevitable death approaching a man whose time has arrived. Karna could do nothing but turn towards that irresistible weapon as it caught him on the neck and severed his head. He dropped to the earth like a mountain toppling over. Just as he fell, his father the sun went in grief to the western hills and vanished from sight. A great cheer went up from the Pandavas. Their most terrible enemy was finally dead. Slowly they withdrew for the day, the Pandavas in great joy and the Kauravas afflicted with unbearable sorrow.

Karna
Oil on Canvas, 250 x 180 cm

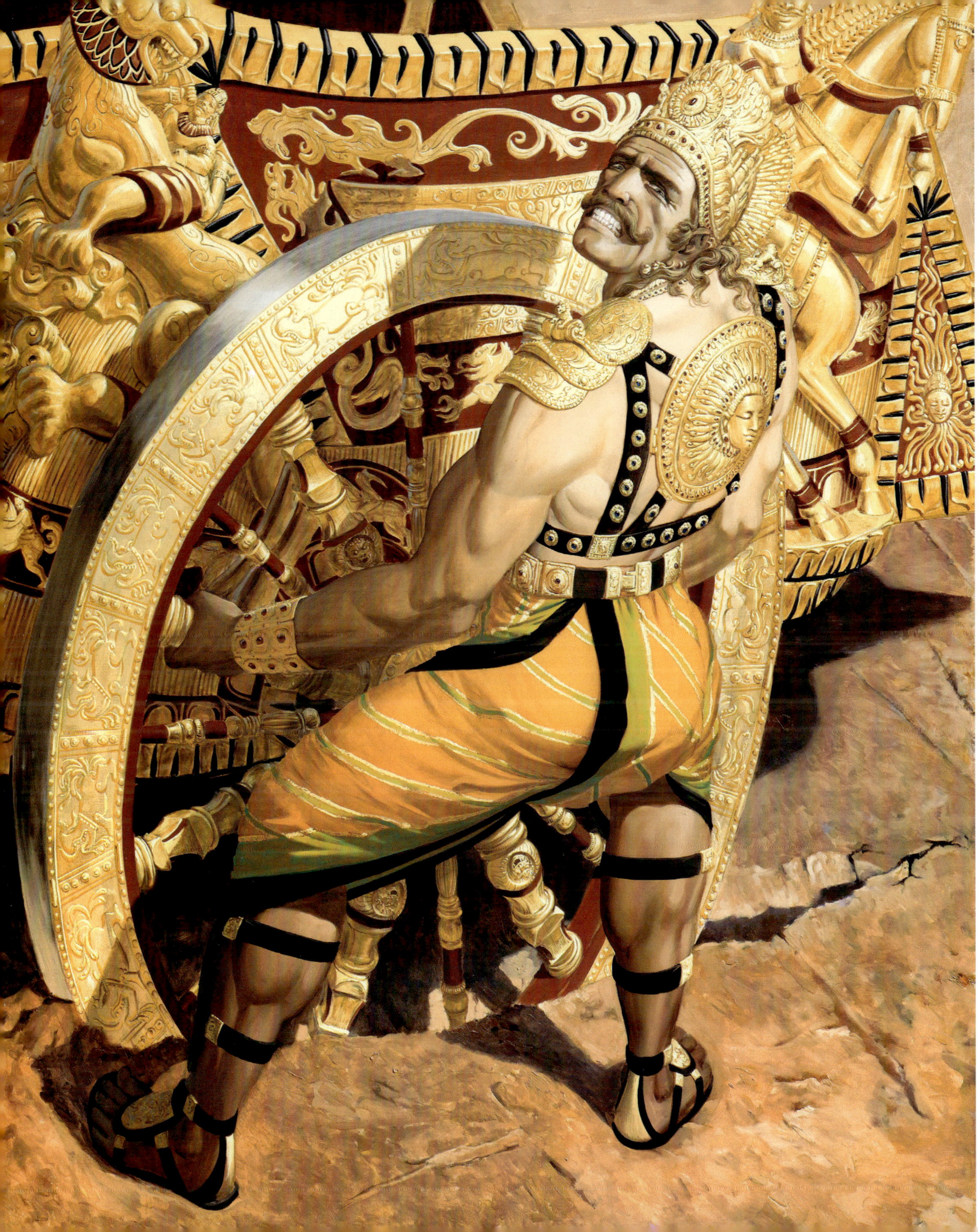

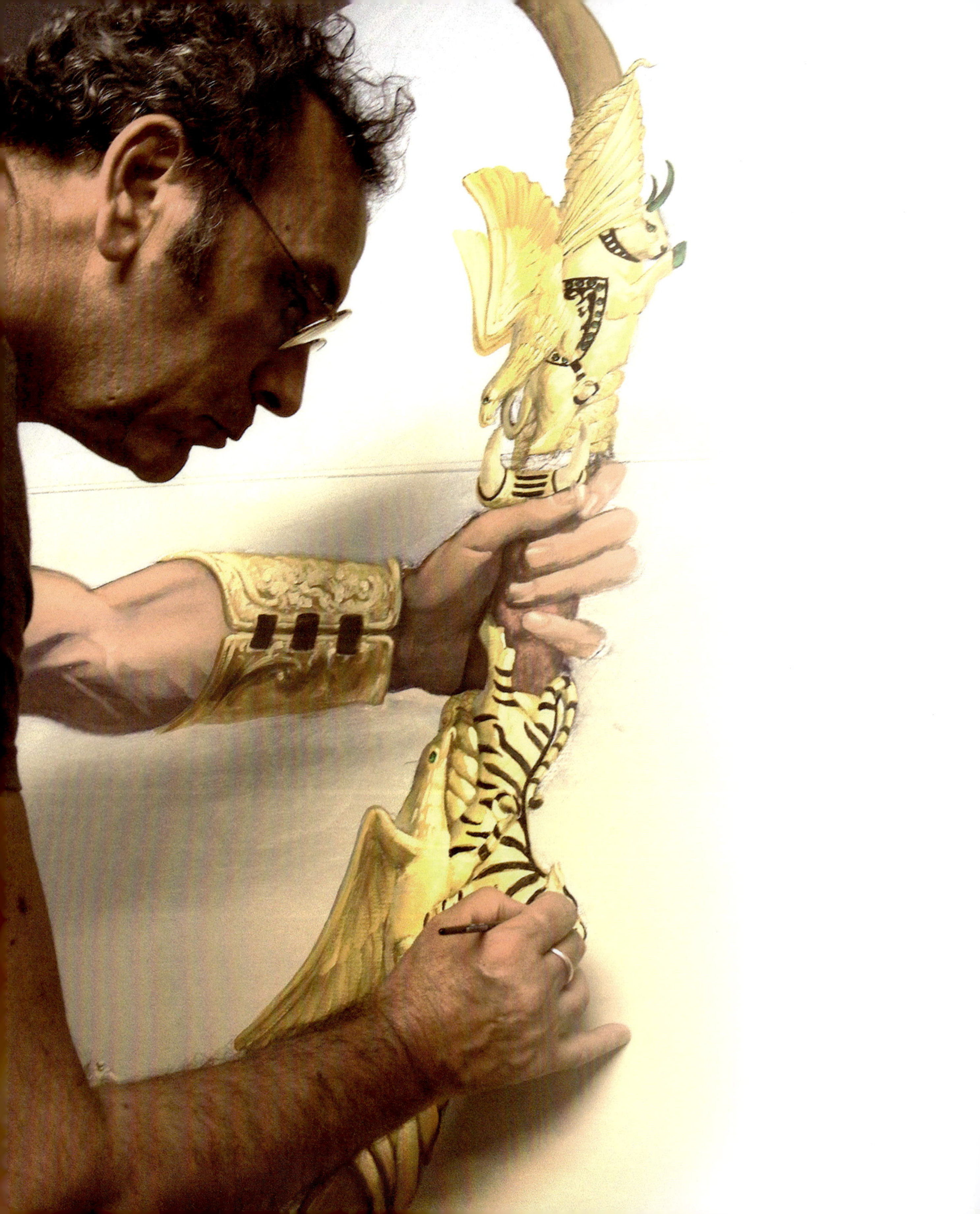

GIAMPAOLO TOMASSETTI

(Jnananjana Dasa)

Giampaolo Tomassetti, or Jnananjana Dasa, was born on March 8, 1955, in Terni, Italy. From 1980 to 1987, he was a founding member of the International Vedic Art Academy, located at Villa Vrindavan in Italy. A number of his paintings appear in books published by the Bhaktivedanta Book Trust. He has held about thirty exhibitions all around Italy. One of his great loves is painting frescoes and walls. He worked on the Mahabharata project for the last twelve years in Città di Castello, Perugia, Italy.

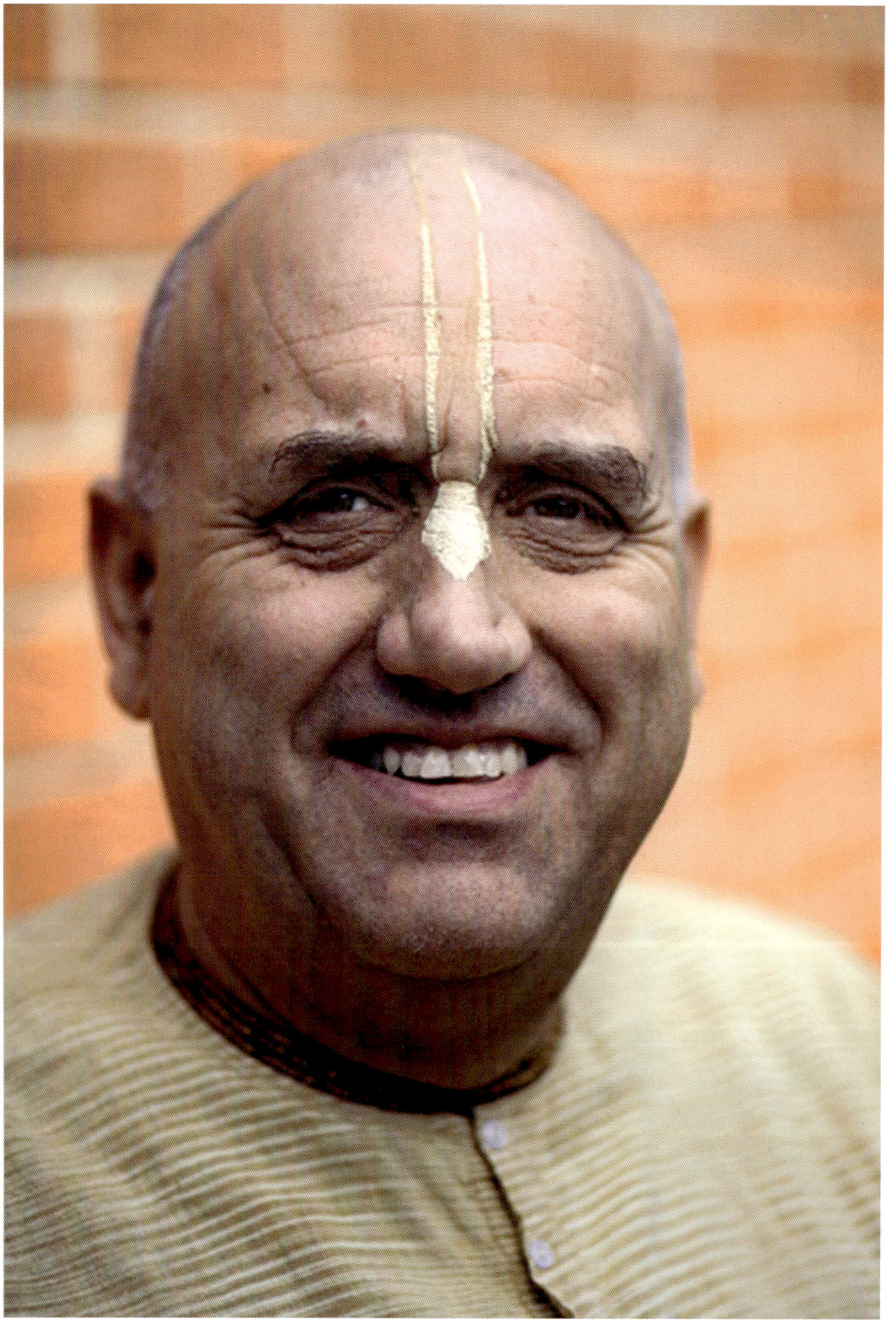

KRISHNA DHARMA

Krishna Dharma lives in England with his wife, Cintamani, and three children: Madhva, Radhika, and Janaki. He is the author of a number of English retellings of ancient Indian classics, including Mahabharata, Ramayana, and Panchatantra. He is also a regular guest broadcaster on the BBC's Pause For Thought. He writes many articles on current events from the Vedic perspective, as a student of His Divine Grace A. C. Bhaktivedanta Swami Prabhupada, the Founder-Acharya of the International Society for Krishna Consciousness. Prabhupada is the author of acclaimed English translations of and commentaries on the Bhagavad-gita, Srimad Bhagavatam, and Sri Caitanya-caritamrta. Krishna Dharma's aim is to make these teachings accessible and relevant to today's world. His motto is "Spiritual Solutions for Material Problems," which sums up his mission of addressing the multitude of society's problems with the profound teachings of ancient sages.

Contributors

Sushma K. Bahl (Delhi) is the author of 5000 *Years of Indian Art* and former head of Arts & Culture for the British Council India. She is also an independent arts adviser, writer and curator and organizes festivals and cultural projects internationally. Sushma was involved with the Triennale-India (guest director), Bharat Rang Mahotsav (project consultant), Asian Art Biennale-Bangladesh (jury member) and ASEAN artists' residency & exhibition-India (curator). The art exhibition Ways of Seeing she curated won the IHC Art India Award.

Prof. Lokesh Chandra was born in India in 1927 at Ambala, Haryana, in an illustrious family of educators. He is the Honorary Director of the International Academy of Indian Culture. Previously he was Chairman of the Indian Council for Historical Research and the Vice-President of the Indian Council for Cultural Relations. He was a Member of Parliament (Rajya Sabha) for two terms (1974-80 and 1980-86). In 2006 the Government of India gave him the Padma Bhushan award, one of the most prestigious civilian honours, for his contributions to academic life and public discourse. He has 596 works and text editions to his credit. Among them are classics like the Tibetan-Sanskrit Dictionary, Materials for a History of Tibetan Literature, Buddhist Iconography of Tibet, and his Dictionary of Buddhist Art in fifteen volumes. He now is writing on the cultural exchanges of the last two millenia between India and China. He has traveled widely in Europe, Asia, and Russia.

Editing: Tom J. Guild

Design: Phelelani Mdabe